D0897626

Learning Practical FinTech from Successful Companies

YOSHITAKA KITAO

WILEY

Contents

Preface

Because I would like this book to be different than introductory books written by academics and commentators in the field of finance, I have focused on corporate managers that struggle day and night to bring about a FinTech revolution.

I consider these people warriors trying to achieve this revolution. I decided to have these warriors (managers) describe their visions of the future and candidly write about what types of strategies and weapons (technologies) they will use to realize them. I am not an editor and have not given contributors to this book any instructions or expressed my opinion to them in advance.

I wrote Chapters 1 and 2 and decided to make these chapters extremely strategic and practical because I am a part of the SBI Group management. I did not have other contributors read my drafts because I did not want them to feel influenced by them.

Even when the drafts for all chapters were completed, I purposefully put off writing the preface because I waited with bated breath for the appearance of concrete evidence that indicates how close this revolution is to affecting all of us.

That evidence is the successful completion of a verification test conducted by a certain consortium. The results were announced on March 2, 2017, and were widely covered by various media outlets the following day. Efforts were led by the Japan Bank Consortium, of which 42 banks (61 banks as of the end of December 2017), more than one-third of Japanese banks, are members. This group successfully conducted a verification test of RC Cloud, a settlement platform that makes use of blockchain technology for low-value, high-frequency payments, and is working to commercialize the platform within this year.

This platform is a cloud-hosted next-generation settlement infrastructure developed by US-based Ripple Labs Inc., an SBI joint venture partner, and is the first such platform in the world. The platform makes it possible to make low-cost (about one-tenth of traditional costs) payments in near real time. Work is currently underway to develop a payment app for mobile devices, and a true payment revolution is set to occur in 2018.

This coincides with the dramatic growth of the robo-advisory service offered by WealthNavi Inc. in partnership with SBI SECURITIES. Applications for accounts exceeded 37,000 in only a little more than a year since the service was launched at the end of January 2017, and customers have deposited more than 28.1 billion yen in assets.

These two developments definitively show that unless financial institutions are quick to introduce the latest technology and increase customer convenience, they will become less competitive and find it difficult to survive.

All financial institutions must be aware that the FinTech revolution will have an impact that vastly exceeds that of the Internet revolution. Our customers are also sure to abandon loyalty to traditional individual financial institutions and become extremely focused on increasing their own benefits.

There will probably be a steady outflow of customers from financial institutions that cannot quickly adapt, and the existing financial order will be destroyed within a short time. This will add to the financial revolution that is occurring simultaneously throughout the world.

The 17 managers who contributed to this book, including myself, have renewed our resolution to write our own future, and we are confident that the full realization of this revolution will be for the good of all people.

I would like to express my deep appreciation to all those who were involved in publishing this book.

Yoshitaka Kitao

Contributors

Yoshitaka Kitao, Representative Director, President, and CEO
SBI Holdings, Inc.
(Preface, Chapter 1, Chapter 2, and Chapter 3)

Kazuhisa Shibayama, Founder and CEO
WealthNavi Inc.
(Chapter 4)

Yosuke Tsuji, Cofounder and CEO
Money Forward, Inc.
(Chapter 4)

Hiroki Maruyama, Cofounder and Representative Director
infcurion group, Inc.
(Chapter 4)

Masami Komatsu, Founder and CEO
Music Securities, Inc.
(Chapter 4)

Yuta Tsuruoka, CEO
BASE, Inc.
(Chapter 4)

Russell Cummer, President and Representative Director
Exchange Corporation K.K.
(Chapter 4)

Yoshiki Yasui, Founder and CEO
Origami Inc.
(Chapter 4)

Yasuhiro Kuda, CEO
Liquid Inc.
(Chapter 4)

Kariya Kayamori, Cofounder and CEO
QUOINE Pte. Ltd.
(Chapter 4)

Takashi Okita, Representative Director
SBI Ripple Asia Co., Ltd.
(Chapter 4)

David E. Rutter, CEO
R3
(Chapter 4)

Hironobu Yoshikawa, CEO and Founder
Treasure Data Inc.
(Chapter 4)

Tomohiro Amino, Representative Director and CEO
GiXo Ltd.
(Chapter 4)

Ryosuke Konishi, Representative Director and CEO/CTO
Generic Solution Corporation
(Chapter 4)

Daisuke Sasaki, Representative Officer
freee K.K.
(Chapter 4)

Naofumi Tsuchiya, President and CEO
Goodpatch Inc.
(Chapter 4)

Kiyokazu Okubo, Executive Officer
SBI Investment Co., Ltd.
(Chapter 5)

Tsutomu Fujita, Professor
SBI Graduate School
(Chapter 5)

Heizo Takenaka
Professor of Faculty of Regional Development Studies at Toyo University
Emeritus Professor at Keio University
(Afterword)

Planning/Editing Staff of the SBI Group

Takeshi Goto, Executive Vice President and Director
  SBI Investment Co., Ltd.

Masato Tanaka, Deputy General Manager, Investment Department
  SBI Investment Co., Ltd.

CHAPTER 1

Internet Revolution and Evolution of FinTech

Paradigm Shift from FinTech 1.0

In 1999, some friends and I published a book called *Challenges of E-Finance* (Toyo Keizai Inc.). In the introduction, I wrote the following:

> *As Schumpeter's words clearly indicate, the new markets, new organizational forms of industries and other products that the Internet gives birth to will probably result in a process of creative destruction that occurs on a global scale, and at a speed that humanity has never seen before. This process will occur first in the finance industry, because that industry is well suited for the Internet.*
>
> *The various companies in our financial group hope to create a stir that shifts Japan's distorted financial system to one that makes it possible to provide greater economic efficiency and convenience to investors and consumers of various financial services, by making use of the Internet's massive destructive power and reforming that distorted financial system. As history has shown, the process of creative destruction does not necessarily have a negative impact on the national economy, but probably has a positive impact when looked at from the long term, and comprehensively. We firmly believe this, and will take on the challenge of transforming the existing financial industry.*

Over the years, I have repeatedly and assertively espoused an Internet revolution of this nature, and have intently pressed forward with efforts to achieve its realization. I will discuss the results of these efforts later, but there is probably wide agreement that this process of creative destruction has progressed with the speed and force that I envisioned when I first wrote the quoted passage.

Advent of FinTech 1.0

Since its founding in 1999, the SBI Group has built the world's first ecosystem for the Internet financial services industry, which includes services such as banking, securities, and insurance. I call this ecosystem *FinTech 1.0*. In Japan, the term *FinTech* started to be used frequently in 2015.

However, US focus had turned to FinTech about two or three years earlier, and it has gradually taken the spotlight. What many people mean by the term *FinTech* is not simply introducing online versions of traditional financial services. Instead, the term applies to the provision of new solutions for the full range of financial services. US-based PayPal Holdings Inc. (among others) took the lead in this movement. Founded in 1998, PayPal provides a payment service that makes use of email accounts and other Internet tools, and, as of October 2017, the number of PayPal subscribers had reached 218 million. If users register their credit card information with PayPal in advance, they can pay for their online shopping at a low cost, and without providing credit card data to online stores, by simply entering their PayPal ID and password and processing their purchases through this platform.

PayPal has brought a welcome breath of fresh air to traditional payment systems. Following PayPal, Apple announced Apple Pay in 2014: a payment system that makes use of the iPhone. Alipay, the payment service that China-based Alibaba Group launched in 2004, is the largest online payment service in the world and boasts at least 500 million users.

Spurred on by PayPal's success, non-financial startup companies – not only payment systems, but also loans, asset management, fund-raising, and remittances across various financial fields globally – have emerged. These individual technologies developed by both startup and established companies are now being applied in the field of finance, and various component technologies owned by different startup companies are being combined and used, primarily by financial institutions that provide full lines of financial products.

FinTech 1.5 : The Result of New Technology

These technologies have fostered development and deployment of efficient and effective financial products in various financial fields. Component technologies include artificial intelligence (AI), big data applications, the evolution of the Internet of Things (IoT, which connects the physical world to the Internet), and robotics. The Japanese financial services industry began using these technologies – individually and in combination – about 2010. The introduction of these technologies rapidly evolved precisely when a

Kondratieff wave (economic cycle that lasts 50–60 years caused by techno-logical innovation) emerged, and major financial institutions began broad-scale deployment in 2012–2013. I refer to this trend, which has attracted attention since 2012–2013, as *FinTech 1.5* because it is basically a more evolved form of FinTech 1.0 (Figure 1.1).

The world that I call *FinTech 2.0* resides in a different dimension than that of the worlds of FinTech 1.0 or FinTech 1.5. The existence of the Inter-net is indispensable to both FinTech 1.0 and FinTech 1.5, and in the world of FinTech 1.0, the World Wide Web, made it possible for individuals to freely exchange various types of data on a larger scale than ever before in human history.

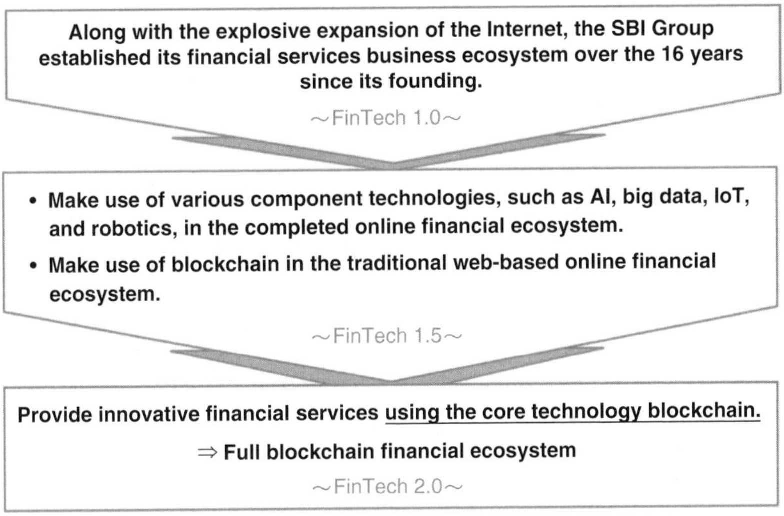

> **Along with the explosive expansion of the Internet, the SBI Group established its financial services business ecosystem over the 16 years since its founding.**
>
> ~FinTech 1.0~

> • **Make use of various component technologies, such as AI, big data, IoT, and robotics, in the completed online financial ecosystem.**
> • **Make use of blockchain in the traditional web-based online financial ecosystem.**
>
> ~FinTech 1.5~

> **Provide innovative financial services <u>using the core technology blockchain</u>.**
> ⇒ **Full blockchain financial ecosystem**
>
> ~FinTech 2.0~

FIGURE 1.1 Evolution of FinTech
Source: SBI Holdings.

In recent years, a vast array of web-based applications (apps) have been developed, and it can be argued that the combination of their commercial availability and greater use of mobile phones has enabled the worlds of FinTech 1.0 and FinTech 1.5 to develop and flourish. However, with respect to financial services, it can be argued–particularly in Japan–that we now live in the world of FinTech 1.0, a composite of online financial services that developed between 1995 and 2000, and the more-evolved system developed primarily by startup companies. For Japanese financial institu-tions, I would observe that their basic business has not evolved since the previous IT era.

Blockchain-based FinTech 2.0

The core technology of FinTech 2.0 is blockchain technology, and unlike FinTech 1.0 and 1.5, FinTech 2.0 does not necessarily rely entirely on the web. The advent of the Internet-based web has made it possible to exchange information throughout the world, but blockchain technology makes a global value exchange over the Internet possible. Both can exist, but they are of different natures and must be treated accordingly (Figure 1.2).

I differentiate among FinTech 1.0, 1.5, and 2.0 because if they are lumped together under the heading FinTech, there is the danger that the innovation potential and its prospects for transforming society may be underestimated. If so, it could hinder the development of blockchain technology in Japan. Since Satoshi Nakamoto published his paper on the cryptocurrency Bitcoin in 2009,[1] blockchain technology has drawn the spotlight as the basic technology underlying Bitcoin.

Although this is only natural considering the growth of blockchain, the focus of the concept has been by and large limited to currency-related functions, as a medium of exchange and store of value. Since about 2012–2013, however, there have been major improvements to not only cryptocurrency frameworks but also business mechanisms (not simply those related to finance), and there has been greater awareness and expectation for the broad application of blockchain, including in the field of public administration.

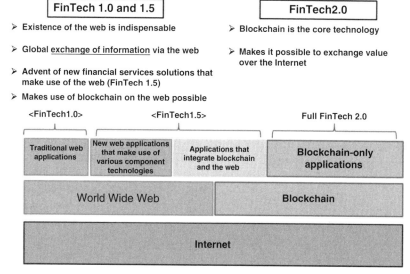

FIGURE 1.2 The World of FinTech 2.0
Source: SBI Holdings.

---

[1] https://Bitcoin.org/Bitcoin.pdf

During this time, one blockchain application after another began to be developed. These apps not only make use of blockchain, but are also used in combination with existing web apps. This means that blockchain technology is not only an entirely new toolkit, but also one that complements existing technologies and may be able to replace them.

Therefore, I would like to touch on the elemental and functional components of blockchain. Different people define blockchain in different ways. There are divergent definitions because blockchains have various important functions. For example, many describe blockchain as a distributed transaction ledger. This is probably a good general definition. Structurally, a blockchain is the foundation of peer-to-peer networks constructed on the Internet and can be called a fully distributed cloud system.

It can also probably be referred to as a platform that makes it possible to securely process various types of transactions involving digital assets. Furthermore, blockchains can function as databases. Network participants (nodes) store and manage transaction history records in a distributed manner using a type of storage site referred to as a *block*.

Finally, blockchain technology can be considered the basic architecture supporting cryptocurrencies. Because blockchain technology was first used as the superstructure for the cryptocurrency Bitcoin, many people now have this image of blockchain technology. Bitcoin is a secured cryptocurrency because of an innovative mechanism, referred to as *proof of work*, which is based on a distributed consensus algorithm for gaining approval through competition between nodes.

It is evident that blockchain can be defined from various perspectives. Since its introduction, the technology has further evolved, and includes the creation of many apps.

One such application, and an extremely important one, is a concept called the *smart contract*: a mechanism that transforms private contracts between parties into a program on a blockchain, and then automatically executes associated contract terms. The arrival of these types of contracts can arguably be deemed a revolutionary upgrade cycle, comparable, in terms of impact, to the development of HTML (hypertext markup language), which made it possible to freely communicate information and create links to the web. The advent of smart contracts eliminates the need for many manual operations that accompany traditional transactions, which currently entail massive costs and amounts of time.

As more and more blockchain apps are developed, related problems, such as expandability, will also quickly be resolved.

Practical Strategy for the Financial Industry

Let's look at a future practical strategy for the financial industry, taking into consideration the availability in the near future of various technologies that can be used in the short term. Here, I will explain the details, using the SBI Group (referred to hereinafter simply as *SBI*) as an example.

In phase one of this development SBI will introduce technologies and services newly developed for the financial ecosystem that it created (FinTech 1.0) and, as a result, will promote the changeover to FinTech 1.5. Because many of these technologies are developed by Japanese and overseas startup companies, SBI established the FinTech Fund to gain access to them. Through this fund, SBI is investing in leading startup companies in various technical fields that possess component technology.

In phase two, the group will introduce the various technologies of FinTech 1.5 into the financial services business ecosystem, striving to increase customer convenience and establish a competitive advantage.

In phase three, SBI will conduct verification tests that make use of FinTech 2.0 technology (i.e., blockchain) in various financial services fields. Of course, it will be necessary to fully understand in which fields those technologies can be used and whether they will lead to incremental efficiencies in transactions processing. At the present time, effective use can probably be made of blockchain in the following financial services fields:

- Bond transactions
- Derivative transactions
- Swap transactions
- Commodity transactions
- Over-the-counter market
- Repo market
- Cryptocurrency transactions

In addition to using blockchain in these fields, the primary goal for numerous financial institutions to distribute the technology is to reduce costs. For example, banks linking operations to a blockchain-based distributed network of cryptocurrencies should dramatically reduce costs for routine financial services operations, such as deposits, withdrawals, remittances, and borrowing of funds through a standalone wallet. Even in the field of insurance, benefit payments will probably be automated with smart contracts. Extensive use of these may be made within the next one to two years.

In the final phase, the use of blockchain and virtual currencies will lead to the creation of global links through cooperation with major partners – in Japan of course, but also throughout the world.

SBI has taken several steps because of its awareness of blockchain's global links and global standards. These actions have included investing in the US-based Ripple Labs Inc., establishing the joint venture SBI Ripple Asia with Ripple Labs Inc., as well as becoming a member of the consortium led by US-based R3 Limited, a company of which it became the main outside shareholder. Unfortunately, since they lack experience, it is difficult for Japanese companies to take the lead in constructing international networks. They can, however, participate in and make use of these networks. Particularly in Asia, SBI will make effective use of SBI Ripple Asia in order to work with local partners in each of the continent's countries, develop an appropriate network, and establish it as that region's component of the international system. This will make it possible to provide a venue for the active participation of startup companies in which the fund invests.

Financial Ecosystem and Strategic Advantage

It is possible to undertake this process in sequence or in parallel, because SBI has a subsidiary – SBI Investment – the responsibility of which is to invest in and assist in the development of startup companies. It is precisely SBI's financial services business ecosystem and organizational linkages with SBI Investment that creates such a strong strategic advantage.

Furthermore, SBI Investment is unique in it that it is not a simple venture capital firm; rather it concentrates in investing in the fields of the Internet and biotechnology and employs numerous experts with abundant experience in such work. These experts identify companies in which SBI can invest at an appropriate price. Once SBI is a shareholder, it provides support on various fronts, with the ultimate objective of placing the company in a position to go public. SBI's greatest support comes in the form of paying for technologies, services, and products offered by these startup companies, enabling organizations across the Group's business ecosystem to use in their own businesses. This process is accretive to the investee companies' earnings in a direct way. Because SBI's business ecosystem comprehensively provides a full range of financial services, such as banking, securities, and insurance, SBI is able to support its investee companies in a sustainable way.

Furthermore, because many of the companies that inhabit the worlds of FinTech 1.5 and 2.0 are startups, their business foundations are extremely fragile. Although regrettable, it is common, therefore, for these companies to fail not because of their value proposition, but rather because they lack the financial resources to achieve monetization.

For many years, SBI has wondered if there is a solution to this problem; that is, if there are measures that benefit sellers, customers, and society that are good for not only SBI and startup companies, but also the customers of important SBI companies.

In regard to this, the following strategies appear appropriate:

1. Construct a financial services business ecosystem.
2. Invest in and partner with startup companies to develop a network of compatible technologies in conjunction with the component companies of the business ecosystem. This includes considering the use case and conducting empirical analyses to develop startup companies' technologies.
3. Bring the appropriate applications to market in order to increase the earnings of the companies we invest in, as well as those of each component company of our business ecosystem.

There are many ways to implement this strategy. For example, SBI can seek to combine component technologies developed by numerous startup companies. There are cases when more than one technology is needed to create a viable financial product, which means you need to combine technologies to develop powerful products.

With participating startup companies, SBI will create these combinations by bringing together the wisdom of the project team members. An extremely important challenge is to find ways to reduce the cost of technology introduction. We believe that expanding sales of financial products developed by numerous strategic partners using the same technology and apps will make it possible to dramatically reduce introduction costs. In order to accomplish that, SBI is trying to establish strategic partnerships with numerous regional financial institutions. SBI also shares the cost of introducing new technologies and developing products with its partners, which results in making it easier to introduce new technologies.

This methodology has come to be referred to as *open innovation* in recent years, and although it is a stylish term, it is not easy to implement. Someone must be the architect. I call people and organizations who do this *mechanism architects*. For us, the architected strategy is summarized by the previous list of three strategies.

In simple terms, my business strategy is to create mechanisms to win. Among these are one to generate a competitive advantage using organizational strategy; an organizational mechanism to both operate the ecosystem and conduct venture capital investment within the same group; a mechanism to realize open innovation; and a mechanism for establishing strategic alliances and partnerships.

Consider the following passage from Sun Tzu's *The Art of War*: "Now the general who wins a battle makes many calculations in his temple ere the battle is fought. The general who loses a battle makes but few calculations beforehand."

This "temple" is the sanctuary where ancestors are enshrined, and in ancient China, it was common to develop battle plans in such spaces. It is impossible to win an actual battle if victory cannot be envisioned when working out a strategy. It is often true that many calculations lead to victory while few calculations lead to defeat.

In Chapter 2, I provide a concise review of the FinTech 1.0 era that SBI has created over the past 16 years. In doing so, I consider the positive impact on competitive advantage and speed of growth of our financial service business ecosystem has had on expanding our customer base and business.

Of course, synergies generated from the discussed ecosystem have already generated significant benefit, making dramatic contributions to SBI's rapid growth up to now. For example, the synergies generated within the securities business and its supporting companies, such as Morningstar Japan (which provides ratings for securities and investment trusts) and SBI Liquidity Market (which provides an over-the-counter market for foreign exchange), have led to the dramatic growth of SBI SECURITIES.

We hope and expect that the ecosystem that SBI has built up will make prominent contributions to the world's migration toward FinTech 1.5 and 2.0. In order to generate further innovations, SBI will consolidate blockchain in its web-based ecosystem, while also considering the establishment of a new ecosystem that uses blockchain as its core technology. At some time in the future, it will be possible to completely switch over.

In the latter part of Chapter 2, I discuss in detail what efforts the overall Group and each Group company are making now.

Evolution of the SBI Group

Accomplishments During the FinTech 1.0 Era

Complexity Knowledge and Business Ecosystem

First, I would like to discuss SBI's efforts during the FinTech 1.0 era.

SBI is primarily a financial services enterprise. It started with a securities business in 1999, then expanded into the banking business in 2007, the casualty insurance business in 2008, and the life insurance business in 2015. In 2016, the company completed the development of an ecosystem for its financial services business, the main channel for which is the Internet. This ecosystem includes various businesses offering services such as payments and remittances. It can also be argued that SBI was the engine that drove the development of online finance in Japan in the 2000s, the decade of the Internet.

Since that time, competition in the Internet era has been qualitatively different. It was my opinion that this competition would migrate to one of network versus network, and that as such, structural differentiation would become extremely important.

The logical business strategy, therefore, was to increase customer satisfaction, strengthen our competitive advantage, and build a dominant customer base. I have read many books and papers on management and worked to apply their principals in the development of the organization. As a result, I have identified the following two major propositions found in the concept of complexity knowledge:

1. The whole should be geared towards the objective of being greater than the sum of the parts.
2. The whole should have new qualities that an individual part cannot achieve.

I also have determined that it may be possible to make use of the concept of business ecosystems, which US academic James F. Moore spelled out in an article published in the *Harvard Business Review* in May–June 1993, "Predators and Prey: A New Ecology of Competition." These two propositions, complexity knowledge and Moore's concept of the business ecosystem, determined the growth direction that SBI has adopted.

A business ecosystem is a commercial community supported by a foundation of organizations and individuals that interact productively with one another. In effective business ecosystems, each company generates synergies and achieves mutual evolution as part of a superstructure that straddles multiple industries. Because of these benefits, companies are able to outperform their rivals. For the same reasons, SBI was able to achieve dramatic growth.

SBI's current main businesses are in financial services, asset management, and biotechnology. In the financial services business ecosystem, SBI's securities, banking, and insurance services have been positioned as its core businesses. Here, SBI has thoroughly pursued synergies within the Group that take the following three forms:

1. Synergies *within* core businesses (securities, banking, and insurance)
2. Synergies *between* core businesses
3. Synergies *with* each business segment (financial services, asset management, and biotechnology)

An example of synergies within core businesses follows. The group of business companies that support SBI SECURITIES, a core business, include SBI Liquidity Market, which provides market infrastructure for the trading of currency pairs; Morningstar Japan, which provides ratings of investment trusts and various other types of financial information; and SBI Asset Management, which develops investment trust products. These companies not only cross-sell but they also work together to provide a wide range of product offerings through SBI SECURITIES. Owing to this, SBI SECURITIES was able to increase its competitiveness, and now boasts the largest customer base in the online securities industry. In addition, the company was the first online securities company to accumulate more than 4.2 million accounts and 12 trillion yen in deposited assets.

Turning to synergies between core businesses, consider the relationship between our banking (SBI Sumishin Net Bank) and securities (SBI SECURITIES) businesses. SBI SECURITIES' dominant customer base contributed to SBI Sumishin Net Bank's growth, in part due to the incremental conveniences associated with aggregation functionality, SBI Hybrid Deposits (the balance of SBI SECURITIES' dedicated bank accounts can be used to purchase cash instruments, such as stocks at SBI SECURITIES), and so on. Therefore, SBI Sumishin

Net Bank was able to generate a profit in its third fiscal year of operation. The current balance of deposits surpasses 4.5 trillion yen, the largest yen balances in the online banking industry.

Synergies with each business segment involve interactions between the financial services business and other business segments, such as asset management and the biotechnology-related business. For example, the asset-management business makes focused investments in the IT field, which contributes to the use of IT-related technologies and know-how possessed by investee companies in the financial services business. However, operating financial services businesses whose main channel is the Internet, along with a deepening knowledge of IT, contributed to improving the asset-management business's ability to judge investments and grow companies that it had invested in.

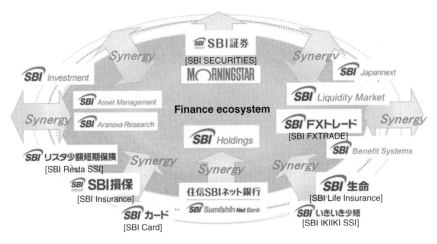

FIGURE 2.1 SBI Group's Financial Ecosystem (FinTech 1.0)
Source: SBI Holdings.

This has resulted in better investments for funds created since the 1990s, which have boasted an average annualized internal rate of return (IRR) for investors of 13.1%.

Because we thoroughly pursued synergies in this way, since its inception in 1999, SBI has been able to establish Fintech 1.0: an Internet financial conglomerate the likes of which the world had never seen (Figure 2.1). This financial ecosystem (FinTech 1.0) was completed in 2016, which was also a point when dramatic changes began to take place in our business environment, including the increasing emergence of FinTech startup companies. As these changes were taking place, it was necessary to promptly transition to FinTech 1.5, and then FinTech 2.0: the next step for SBI.

The definitions of FinTech 1.0, 1.5, and 2.0 are given in Chapter 1, and SBI will complete the process of transitioning from the current FinTech 1.0 era to the FinTech 1.5 and 2.0 eras. In the next section, I discuss the organizational response and actual efforts of each company to further evolve the completed finance ecosystem associated with these new technologies.

Group Strategy to Promote the Shift to FinTech 1.5 and FinTech 2.0

Big Data Office

In August 2012, SBI Holdings initiated a group-wide project and established the big data office. At that time, hardware performance and software processing technology were improving, a wider range of device choices were available, and new technologies and services were being introduced. Against this backdrop, efforts to perform analyses on large-volumes of various data (so-called big data) to achieve operational improvements, and enhance customer service, marketing, and product development accelerated, particularly in the United States.

At the same time, Japan was being introduced to the term *big data*, and I believed that even in the financial industry, in the near future, the key to each company's destiny would be whether it could make effective use of the concept. We therefore decided that it was necessary to collect and analyze data obtained from our customer base, which surpassed 13 million at that time (23 million as of now), including massive transaction histories and access logs. In doing so, we were exceedingly mindful of the need to properly handle personal information, while at the same time seeking to improve operations, raise customer service levels and increase marketing efficiencies of the various Group companies. This action was an essential element of our customer-centric principle, and helped us to establish a competitive advantage.

We established big data offices in the our companies with customer bases composed of typical consumers and in the business departments within SBI Holdings, and we staffed these offices as we deemed appropriate. These offices took the lead in introducing multi-purpose tools (including log analysis and Internet ad distribution). In addition, they establish marketing metrics based on data collected in partnership with the various Group companies. Beyond this, they are involved in the management of processes including marketing, ad expense management, and promoting selling across Group companies. I often attend the big data meetings held within and across Group companies and SBI Holdings' business departments in order to reinforce the high priority I place on these initiatives.

By way of offering some context respecting SBI's big data footprint, I offer the following statistics (current as of November 2017):

- Group website page views: 940 million pages viewed per month
- Ad data for 34 companies
- Data on 1.1 billion transactions per month
- Behavior history (access log for 40 sites)
- Analysis platform (46 TB stored on Hadoop)

Blockchain Promotion Department

As noted in Chapter 1, I believe that blockchain technology will be responsible for the greatest evolution in the history of the finance industry.

In February 2016, SBI Holdings established the Blockchain Promotion Department to undertake various activities, some of which are listed below:

- Supporting the development of proof of concept (PoC), and introducing a pilot version in order to verify the technology developed under our joint venture with Ripple Labs Inc.
- Supporting the operation of The Japan Bank Consortium.
- Participating in the international blockchain consortium R3.
- Launching a cryptocurrency business
- Holding blockchain seminars for group members in partnership with Keio University Shonan Fujisawa Campus
- SBI Holdings, SBI BITS, and NEC demonstration test of KYC using blockchain technology
- Development of settlement platform *S Coin Platform* by promoting distributed ledger technology.

We were the first Internet-based financial group to participate in R3, an international blockchain consortium. This US-led association features leading financial institutions from more than 100 countries and is one of the world's largest working groups organized for the purpose of increasing the efficiency of financial markets. We announced our participation in March 2016, following the lead of Mitsubishi UFJ Financial Group, Sumitomo Mitsui Financial Group, Mizuho Financial Group, and Nomura Holdings.

It is meaningless to participate in the working group simply to gather information. We believe it is important that the forum be used to develop written global standards. We must not simply accept things as they are, but also state our opinion, create a network centered on Asia, and then proceed toward standardization on a global basis. If we do not do so, we will not achieve our workflow objectives. It is exactly because of this reality that we are putting all of our energy into these efforts. Furthermore, we quickly decided to invest in R3 and expressed our strong desire to further strengthen our partnership with this company, to make use of blockchains.

The Blockchain Promotion Department is now moving forward with the development of the S Coin Platform, a settlement platform utilizing blockchain-related technology, as well as a cryptocurrency, named S Coin. It is considering leveraging SBI Virtual Currencies, which was established in November 2016 and will offer cryptocoin exchange and trading services. I will discuss SBI Virtual Currencies in the next sections, when I review the efforts being made by the various Group companies.

Establishing Funds

The FinTech Fund

As mentioned in Chapter 1, SBI pioneered the concept of applying a fund construct and using it to invest in promising startup companies as a means of sourcing component technology in the field of FinTech. Established in December 2015, the fund has raised a total of 30.0 billion yen from not only the SoftBank Group and Mizuho Financial Group, but also from about 30 regional financial institutions. Even after the fund-raising was completed, there was incremental demand for fund investment.

A total 23.5 billion yen investment in 68 companies has already been decided (as of December 31, 2017). At the same time, SBI Holdings is also making direct investments and, all told, the overall Group will allocate a total of 38.5 billion yen to investments in the FinTech field.

Because blockchain architecture is the core FinTech technology, our investment process has focused on companies in this field, including US-based Ripple Labs Inc., Korea-based Coinplug Inc., and Japan-based bitFlyer Inc., Orb Inc., and QUOINE Pte. Ltd. Japan.

The fund is also steadily diversifying its investments in fields other than blockchain, and these include big data, payments, cloud funding, and robo-advisors.

The fund does not simply make investments because the goal is to create a competitive advantage for the various SBI financial services companies, through the introduction of innovative technology and services possessed by the startup companies in which we have secured an interest. Furthermore, SBI will provide support to financial institutions that invested in the fund, through the distribution of incremental technical efficiencies developed through the process. In this way, we can contribute to the sales of the various startup companies and, as a result, improve the performance of the FinTech Fund itself.

SBI Regional Bank Value Creation Fund

In January 2018, we also established the SBI Regional Bank Value Creation Fund as a privately placed investment trust, the objective of which is to increase the corporate value of regional banking enterprises. The fund will invest in regional financial institutions to improve corporate governance, and raise corporate value through various efforts such as providing support for the introduction of FinTech.

Furthermore, we hope the investment process will reinvigorate local communities by making use of innovative Internet technologies, such as simple, low-cost electronic commerce platforms for client companies and individual stores of financial institutions in various regions. Following are concrete examples of our planned initiatives in this area:

- Strengthening sourcing capabilities and expanding products offered through a partnership with SBI MONEY PLAZA
- Providing SBI's various asset-management products to affiliated financial institutions and their clients
- Providing overseas investment and financing opportunities by making use of SBI's overseas network
- Proposing new financial businesses that make use of technology possessed by SBI and its FinTech investee companies

Through these efforts, we believe it may be possible to create a new standard banking model for the region.

Through initiatives that fully use these funds, we want to create added value for customers both within and outside of the Group. Specifically, by building win-win relationships with financial institutions in Japan and abroad, and by providing customers within and outside of the Group with composite services that include information, efficient financing, and service frameworks, we believe that all stakeholders in the ecosystem stand to benefit. I refer to this as "expanding network value." Having already established various types of partnerships with financial enterprises in Japan and abroad, including regional financial institutions, SBI will strive to further strengthen those relationships.

Establishing Joint Ventures

SBI Ripple Asia

As information and communication technology (ICT) has undergone revolutionary changes in recent years, so has customer behavior and life as members in society. As a result, the needs related to fund transfers have evolved. They now include demand for around-the-clock, real-time payments and small payments. There have also been major changes in needs related to foreign currencies, because due to cross-border electronic commerce and Japan's increased footprint in Asia, borders are disappearing throughout the world. As for the existing overseas payment infrastructure, however, there were various issues such as length of time it takes to receive funds, high remittance costs, and uncertainty of remittances that must pass through multiple intermediary institutions.

In January 2016, SBI invested in and decided to establish a joint venture with Ripple Labs Inc., in order to promote the creation of an international remittance platform that uses blockchains. Ripple is a promising US-based FinTech startup company that is developing an innovative next-generation payment platform, xCurrent. At present, we are undertaking verification testing for Ripple's solution, which we believe will replace the existing payment infrastructure.

In May 2016, we established SBI Ripple Asia as a joint venture, and began providing a payment platform that uses blockchains in Japan and other Asian countries. SBI has a 10.5% stake in Ripple (as of September 30, 2017), and is working to further strengthen the relationship. Through our partnership with Ripple, and business with SBI Ripple Asia, we feel we are promoting a remittance revolution.

As for efforts within Japan, the Japan Bank Consortium, for which SBI Ripple Asia serves as the secretariat, was launched in partnership with 42 financial institutions, including multiple regional banks, in Japan (61 financial institutions as of December 31, 2017). This consortium is examining new remittance and payment services that make use of various technologies such as blockchain. The verification tests were completed in March 2017, and now the consortium will promote its commercial use at various financial institutions. Entities that move quickly may be able to launch commercial use with aggressive timetables in 2018.

Joint Venture with IBM

As for Japan, the business environment in which regional financial institutions operate is one that faces increasing challenges. In the short term, profits and corporate value will deteriorate because of the negative interest rate policy adopted by the Bank of Japan. Looking further down the road, FinTech startup companies will have a stronger presence, owing to the development and evolution of financial innovations. Finally, in the long term, their business foundation will shrink and deteriorate due to the aging and ultimate decline of its population base.

These widely understood trends have fostered active debate regarding regional financial institutions, and even within the Financial Services Agency, covering topics such as support for industry restructuring and the incentivization of innovation. The know-how and expertise that we have acquired driving the development of online finance in Japan combined with our cooperation with FinTech startups will contribute to the creation of new opportunities for regional financial institutions. This will, in turn, lead to an increase in their corporate value. In undertaking this initiative, we remain very mindful of the challenges that confront us, including, human resource and technical obstacles to regional financial institutions introducing systems developed by FinTech startup companies.

But we feel certain we are on the right track. As a case in point, our know-how and technology related to online financial services caught the eye of IBM Japan, which is building core banking systems for numerous Japanese financial institutions. Collaboration between our two organizations should add efficiency to the critical challenge of introducing FinTech to regional financial institutions.

Though IBM rarely enters into joint ventures, shortly after initiating discussions, SBI and IBM Japan established SBI FinTech Incubation KK, through a joint investment in February 2017. The company is building a FinTech platform to support the introduction of new FinTech services at regional financial institutions and will expand its joint business from there. This FinTech platform, which will link the various services and systems of not only SBI's online financial companies, but also FinTech startup companies both in Japan and abroad (including those in which the Group has invested) will be made available to regional financial institutions. These institutions will be able to select from a wide range of FinTech services, and efforts will be made to promote their smooth introduction. The FinTech platform will link regional financial institutions to startup companies, and lead to a broader use of each company's services, which will raise the corporate value of our investee companies. This, we believe, will foster a virtuous cycle. SBI FinTech Incubation may very well be a revolutionary joint venture.

Strategies of Various Companies in the FinTech 1.5 and 2.0 Era

For our various businesses, we are promoting not only the pursuit of greater client convenience and uniqueness of services but also the introduction of new FinTech technologies at the various Group companies, in order to differentiate them from their competitors. The following section discusses how SBI is promoting the introduction of FinTech and the efforts being made by the main companies.

1. Securities

Robo-advisor service   Since July 2016, SBI SECURITIES has been providing the investment trust selection support tool SBI Fund Robo, which uses a robo-advisor. SBI Fund Robo recommends investment strategies, taking into consideration responses to questions relating to age, investment experience, risk preference and regional preferences. There are currently 2,600 such trusts handled by SBI SECURITIES, each of which is rated by Morningstar Japan rating data.

SBI SECURITIES has also established tie-ups with WealthNavi Inc. and Money Design Co., Ltd., which make use of cutting-edge financial technology to provide a world-class asset management service featuring internationally diversified investments. On January 31 and July 26, 2017, WealthNavi for SBI SECURITIES and THEO + SBI SECURITIES, a customized robo-advisor service, were launched, respectively.

Both companies' robo-advisor service provides support for novice investors through an asset-management service that automates the entire process and creates an optimal portfolio using a highly objective and transparent algorithm. Therefore, individual investors are able to make rational investments that maintain appropriate asset allocation as they continue to make contributions to their portfolio.

SBI SECURITIES allows users to use a single sign-on (SSI) function to log into both companies' websites directly from its own website. Furthermore, SBI is currently examining various other features, including providing a WealthNavi smartphone app linked to existing SBI SECURITIES applications.

Through our next-generation financial technology and our collaboration with WealthNavi and Money Design, we expect to provide cutting-edge asset management services to more individual investors across SBI's dominant customer base.

AI Furthermore, SBI SECURITIES provides a dialogue-based FAQ service that makes use of an AI engine. SBI SECURITIES was the first financial institution to adopt LINE Customer Connect, a customer support service for companies that use the communication app LINE. This service can be used by anyone, free of charge, by adding the newly created SBI SECURITIES Customer Support LINE Official Account as a navigation tool.

For questions regarding SBI SECURITIES' services, such as how to open an account, the technology analyzes and processes the wording of the question using the general-purpose conversation engine Bedore, provided by Bedore KK. Under this framework, the appropriate response is automatically displayed with a high degree of precision.

Bedore includes not only a natural language processing function that can understand clients' questions but also a cutting-edge deep-learning function. It is possible to repeatedly conduct automatic learning by verifying questions and answers, and this further improves the precision of responses. With this service, clients can easily and quickly resolve their questions without even contacting the call center, dramatically improving customer satisfaction (Figure 2.2).

FIGURE 2.2 Dialogue-Based FAQ Service
Source: SBI Holdings.

Blockchain   In cooperation with IBM Japan, SBI recently conducted a verification test of the feasibility and benefits of constructing a securities trading system based on a new distributed platform using blockchain technology. The goal is to quickly commercialize blockchain technology for securities operations.

The verification test involved the vetting of a series of operational processes–ranging from issuing bonds to redeeming them, and it proved to be successful. Specifically, the test confirmed that SBI's automation and sharing of databases verified the prospect of reducing infrastructure costs among related parties and the feasibility of replacing existing operations. It also allowed for the evaluation of blockchains for securities operations and systems.

As a result, SBI is moving forward with the concept of using blockchains in securities operations in a production environment. SBI SECURITIES also participated in a verification test of the use of blockchain technology for securities market infrastructure–jointly conducted by Japan Exchange Group, Inc. and IBM Japan.

2. Investment Trust Rating Agency

Morningstar Japan is developing an investment advisory service using a robo-advisor investment tool. In this endeavor, SBI Fund Robo analyzes user risk tolerance based on answers to questions on factors such as age, annual income, and financial knowledge. The algorithm then suggests the investment trust portfolio appropriate for those clients. Morningstar Japan is the largest investment trust rating agency in Japan, and using the latest rating data, it can propose funds that we feel will sustain a competitive performance advantage.

There are now 16 companies (as of November 30, 2017) that use the robo-advisor management tool offered by Morningstar Japan, and these include SBI SECURITIES, Mizuho Bank, SMBC Nikko Securities, and Asatsu-DK (a defined contribution pension). It is forecasted that, on a worldwide basis, more than 240 trillion yen in assets will be managed by robo-advisors by 2020.

3. Bank

Despite the innovation lags inherent in the banking industry, SBI Sumishin Net Bank was quick to start its work on making use of blockchain in its banking operations. In December 2015, the company launched the first verification test for the use of blockchain for core banking operations in Japan. Here, it worked in the cooperation with Nomura Research Institute (NRI), which possesses significant experience in building systems in the financial field. The test was a success. Routine banking operations range from managing client account balances and interest accruals, processing deposits, withdrawals, fund transfers, remittances, foreign-exchange transactions, payment of funds across financial institutions, and so on. The test results verified the efficacy of the platform from the following perspectives:

- Load resistance (determination as to whether the system can handle the projected volume of transactions associated with 2.5 million accounts without the server going down)
- Resistance to falsification
- Cost-reduction possibilities

The tests confirmed that blockchains are indeed useful from these various perspectives. Of course, there are still issues to be resolved, but work is moving forward to realize the application of blockchains in a banking environment.

Even in fields other than blockchains, SBI Sumishin Net Bank has taken the lead in promoting advanced efforts among its competitors. One of these is expanding its suite of APIs (application programming interfaces, a mechanism for retrieving and using items such as software functions and managed data from another program). Linking a bank API to a FinTech startup company makes it possible to provide breakthrough services, such as offering secure and accurate information on balances and deposits/withdrawals of client accounts, through the usage of services that FinTech startup companies provide (Figure 2.3).

SBI Sumishin Net Bank launched its first API-linked service on March 25, 2016, in collaboration with Money Forward, Inc., a technology company that offers an automated household account book and asset-management service for individuals, and a product called MF Cloud Series for small- and medium-sized enterprises.

Later that year, SBI Sumishin Net Bank introduced an API-linked service with the cloud accounting software provider, freee K.K., and then one with NestEgg Inc., a subsidiary of the infcurion group, which provides the automated savings service finbee. Furthermore, working with WealthNavi, it was possible to undertake identity-confirmation operations using an API link. We also launched a service for small-value asset management linked to credit card payments.

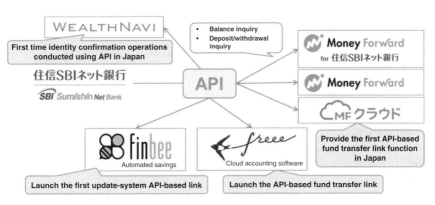

FIGURE 2.3 API Economy
Source: SBI Holdings.

Further details of this service will be discussed in Chapter 4. However, it first bears mention that along with APIs, we are focusing our attention on business loan services based on accounting transactions – again using FinTech constructs. These services feature the timely provision of financing to sole proprietorships and smaller enterprises, through links to cloud accounting frameworks that possess user data such as bank transactions and payment information.

As its first FinTech service, SBI Sumishin Net Bank launched a loan-offering service, Lending 1, for credit card member stores. Here, we worked in collaboration with Zeus, a subsidiary of SBI FinTech Solutions, which provides payment services. This makes it possible to receive financing in time windows as short as the same day. We are currently seeking to expand our network of partner companies, and one such success was our December 2016 announcement of a business partnership with Coiney Inc., which provides a credit payment service, called Coiney, that uses smartphones and tablet devices.

Furthermore, we recently launched a verification test, in partnership with Hitatchi, Ltd., of a cutting-edge loan screening method that utilizes AI and the statistical analysis of data from sources such as global information systems (GISs). The goal here is to increase the speed and precision of loan screening through analysis of not only traditionally used data such as customer age and income, but also other information, including regional economic indicators and changes recorded in the time series of various types of data captured by Hitachi AI Technology/H.

4. Insurance

At the online casualty insurance company SBI Insurance, departments that focus solely on the FinTech strategy are moving forward on various fronts, including the development of more personalized car insurance, the premium for which is calculated based on driving behavior. The company is also examining the use of AI to increase the efficiency of screening operations.

In addition, SBI Life Insurance is advancing the development of more personalized life insurance products in collaboration with FiNC Inc., a mobile health technology startup. On November 30, 2016, an application developed by FiNC to manage health and improve life habits was made available to individuals covered by SBI Life Insurance's whole life medical insurance, called MO. And from July 2017, the application was made available to all policy-holders of the company. The system, which is still in development, is designed to link insured individual's health and medical data (e.g. body mass index, blood pressure, medical data mortality rate, morbidity rate, medical expenses due to this, etc.) to the insurance processing matrix.

Once these data links are in place, it will be possible to accelerate the development of personalized insurance, designed to take into consideration the state of health and efforts to live a healthier life made by each insured person. In turn, this will allow for the more efficient management of premiums, in part by setting lower rates and expanding the scope of coverage to reflect the insured person's efforts to improve their health.

In US or European countries, this field is referred to as InsurTech (Insurance x Technology), and research on new insurance business models is rapidly moving forward. It appears that efforts in the United States and Europe have progressed further than those in Japan. As such, we are now examining the possibility of investing in a US- or Europe-based startup company in this field.

5. FX-Related Business

SBI Liquidity Market is examining the prospects of derivative financial instrument trading using blockchain, with the goal of introducing the technology in 2018. The verification test was conducted in cooperation with SBI BITS, SBI's system development company, and together, we were able to verify the feasibility of a trading platform using blockchain for order matching and account management. A verification test using actual products confirmed the performance that can be obtained by high-frequency derivative trading.

Furthermore, efforts are being made to utilize AI chatbots (programs that automatically answers users' messages) and to analyze and make visible this data – all in partnership with Microsoft Japan. Through these initiatives, we are working to further improve the environment so that FX trading can transpire on the platform – in safety and with peace of mind.

6. Cryptocurrency

In recent years, Bitcoin and other cryptocurrencies have drawn considerable interest from major media and market participants, and these currencies are already actively traded. Furthermore, the governance and regulatory policy picture for handling cryptocurrencies are becoming clear, owing to various developments, including the passage of the amended Payment Services Act in May 2016.

As these environmental changes have unfolded, SBI has decided to enter the business of operating cryptocurrency trading exchanges in order to meet the diverse needs of investors and to provide opportunities to manage assets with new stores of value. In addition to providing cryptocurrency exchange and trading services for the various group companies, SBI Virtual Currencies is planning to steadily expand the type of cryptocurrencies it handles, and develop advance services that make use of cryptocurrencies through tie-ups with cryptocurrency exchanges.

For example, we seek to arrange linkages to cryptocurrency exchanges in Japan and abroad to trade Bitcoin and XRP (US-based Ripple's cryptocurrency) – ultimately to trade tokens issued by the various regions. Our plan is to promote and provide diverse types of exchange and trading services, including that of S Coins, an in-house developed digital asset, with other cryptocurrencies, cash, SBI Points, and bullion. Furthermore, we are examining handling not only coins with a variable value but also those with an exchange value of 1 yen and 1 dollar.

There is now movement to recognize cryptocurrencies as a medium of exchange, and I think that this trend is picking up steam throughout the world. When that happens, SBI Virtual Currencies will take off.

7. Savings Bank

SBI's FinTech efforts are not limited to Japan. For example, Korea-based SBI SAVINGS BANK is moving forward with a project in cooperation with the DAYLI Financial Group, one of SBI's investee companies. They plan to increase the sophistication of SBI SAVINGS BANK's receivables tracking and credit rating models. Composed of numerous Korea-based FinTech startups, the DAYLI Financial Group is a digital financial service company that leads the Korean financial markets. The use of big data solutions for financial institutions that employ machine learning possessed by the DAYLI Intelligence, a member of the DAYLI Financial Group, may make it possible to more precisely estimate customers' credit status. The verification based on existing transaction histories confirmed that it is possible to provide more customers with financing through the development and implementation of higher-precision credit-quality assessment tools that reduce the incidence of default. Through the introduction of the new screening model, the bank's balance of loans increased, and at the same time, the delinquency ratio of those which have been additionally approved to be loaned out has remained at a low level.

CHAPTER 3

Background of the FinTech Revolution

Ascertaining Prospects of Growth Companies

As pioneers in the industry, we established a fund to primarily invest in promising Japanese and overseas startup companies that possess component technology in the field of FinTech (the FinTech Fund).

The distinguishing feature of this fund is that it creates a framework under which it is possible to not simply invest in startup companies but also to support the commercialization of their services in a large ecosystem. It does so by actively making use of their technologies and services at the SBI Group financial services companies and at financial institutions that have invested in the fund.

How does the fund make decisions regarding investments in startup companies? Our process features four key points. They are: (1) target market and customers, (2) management team, (3) business strategy, and (4) terms of the investment. Investment decisions are made by looking comprehensively at all four factors. In this chapter, I will explain the first three.

1. Target Market and Customers

The market a startup company enters is an important factor. We take a careful look at this and analyze various aspects, including growth potential, earnings potential, competitive environment, technical evolution, and structural changes. We consider whether the market will allow the startup company to grow to a certain level even though there may be constraints on resources, such as funds and management personnel. These are critical issues for us. In addition, it is important to ascertain to what extent customers are receptive to the service and product the startup company is providing. It is particularly important for us to determine whether the startup in question is looking at its offering from the end user's perspective, and whether the provided services and products put the customer first.

As for the market in which the startup competes, what types of existing players are providing end users with what types of similar services through what channels and at what price? What are the market issues and complaints of end users? What are the strengths and weaknesses of the service that the startup company is planning on providing, as compared to similar services offered elsewhere?

We analyze these issues from various perspectives. Furthermore, we interview experts who are knowledgeable about the service provided, the management team of Group companies, and sometimes the potential users of the products and services offered.

In mature economies such as Japan, many markets are characterized by fierce competition among numerous competent players in the field. Under these conditions, it is not easy to find markets in which startups can grow. It is necessary to enter these investments with as much certainty as is possible in terms of creating a prominent distinguishing factor, such as a differentiated creative approach or strong technical capability that cannot be easily copied.

2. Management Team

The world of startups is a volatile environment, characterized by mobility among workers and other uncertainties—which can work either for or against a given startup initiative. Under these conditions, managers who possess strong individual qualities, such as the ability to act and execute upon a decision once it has been made, and enough personal appeal to constructively engage various parties including vendors, business partners, and employees, are necessary.

In the field of FinTech, there are numerous regulations, and existing financial institutions are extremely influential in setting their course. Speed is necessary to quickly enter markets created through deregulation and other opportunities; at the same time, engaging existing players (e.g., financial institutions) is also a critical business-building skill. From this perspective, it is important for the leaders of startup companies to firmly understand the financial industry, and possess the experience and skills to create strong, effective relationships with the management of financial institutions.

3. Business Strategy

As discussed previously, in order to achieve success in mature markets characterized by heavy competition, it is important to attack the market with an approach that existing players cannot adopt. In addition to quickly entering the market with the agility that only a startup possesses, it is necessary for startup companies to carefully formulate a business strategy to beat the competition. This can take the form of offering services that make use of cutting-edge technology that existing players struggle to use or a price strategy to which major companies cannot respond.

It is said that there are now almost 300 FinTech startup companies in Japan. Presumably, each of these companies possesses a unique strategy. However, there are probably few that launch their business with a clear path to success. We examine whether the business plans and models created by startup companies are reasonable from two perspectives: that of an investor with almost 20 years of experience in operating venture funds, and that of a financial business operator who has created a unique, forward-facing, global FinTech ecosystem.

In the field of FinTech, for various reasons, it is difficult for startup companies to create a compelling value proposition. These include resourcing issues, the competitive environment in which they operate, and regulatory challenges. It is therefore imperative for us to examine the type of business model and partner strategy they envision. Many startup companies have not taken their business models to the point of completion before they begin to accept investment capital. As necessary and appropriate, we provide support to fill these holes in business planning and execution.

Throughout history, major changes in the structure of various industries have given rise to startup companies. Having considered how to respond to the information revolution that is occurring now, the SBI Group will work with startup companies to create change, as is consistent with our objective to lead the FinTech revolution.

In the next chapter, I will introduce FinTech startup companies that are launching unique businesses that we believe will drive the growth markets of FinTech.

CHAPTER 4

Breakthrough FinTech Companies

Robo-advisor

WealthNavi
   Representative: Kazuhisa Shibayama, Representative Director
   Company profile
      Founded: 2015
      Partners: SBI SECURITIES, SBI Sumishin Net Bank
   With a mission of "creating a society where working people can build wealth," WealthNavi provides each customer with fully automated asset management system tailored to meet his or her individual needs. In October 2016, the company announced a capital alliance with the SBI Group. WealthNavi also provides service for customers of SBI SECURITIES and SBI Sumishin Net Bank.

Yoshitaka Kitao: Tell us about the history of the company.

Kazuhisa Shibayama: WealthNavi endeavors to offer everyone in Japan access to the same level of asset management service enjoyed by wealthy investors around the world. Based on a customer's answers to a few simple questions, we prepare a tailored investment plan, conduct trades, handle additional contributions, and even automatically optimize the portfolio from a tax standpoint.

   Though our April 2015 founding date makes us a relatively new company, we completed our FSA registration (Type I Financial Instruments Business, Investment Management Business, Investment Advising and Agency) in the record time of 8 months. In October 2016, we announced a capital alliance with the SBI Group. WealthNavi has also received investments from not only the Development Bank of Japan, but also the venture capital companies of the three major Japanese banking groups. This makes us one of the most watched FinTech startup companies in the industry.

A Tenfold Difference in Assets

KS: My founding of WealthNavi followed a career featuring tours of
        duty at Japan's Ministry of Finance, a stint at McKinsey & Com-
        pany, and a crash course at programing school, where I indepen-
        dently developed the first prototype for our service.

        At the Ministry of Finance, I was responsible for various opera-
        tions, including social security and the introduction of the Nippon
        Individual Savings Account (NISA) system, but I retired after mar-
        rying an American. Later, when I was working at McKinsey's New
        York office, I was shocked to find out that my parents-in-law in the
        United States had financial assets valued at almost 10 times that of
        my parents in Japan.

        My Japanese parents had stopped trading stocks after the col-
        lapse of the bubble, and most of their financial assets were in the
        form of deposits and insurance. Their financial assets consisted
        only of their pensions and what remained from their retirement
        benefits after paying off their mortgage. However, my American
        in-laws had entrusted their asset management to their companies'
        benefit services and an independent financial planner – whatever
        remained from their salaries after living expenses and their mort-
        gage payments was placed in long-term, internationally diversified
        investments. As a result, my American in-laws had accumulated up
        to several hundred million yen in financial assets, and at one time
        even owned a small private airplane.

        At the time of this discovery, I was supporting institutional inves-
        tors with offices on Wall Street, and spent a year and a half devel-
        oping an algorithm to manage the risk and assets of a portfolio
        valued at about 10 trillion yen. But because my wealth disparity
        discovery, I decided to launch a new company in Japan. Thinking
        "the formula is the same whether it is 10 trillion yen, 1 billion yen,
        or 100 million yen, I should be able to help regular people manage
        their assets in this world-class fashion." I resigned from McKinsey
        and started to study the basics of programming with a group of
        20-somethings at a school in Shibuya. I finished the WealthNavi
        prototype by the time I graduated, and founded the company in
        April 2015.

        Over the little more than two years since then, the number of
        WealthNavi employees has grown to just under 40 full-time profes-
        sionals (more than half are engineers), and the company's capital
        has increased to 2.1 billion yen. With both the regulatory status of
        a financial institution and the technical skills to create something

new, the company has grown into one of Japan's top FinTech startup companies.

Automating the Asset Management Process

KS: WealthNavi's service is fully automated, from setting investment goals to allocating assets to optimizing taxes (Figure 4.1).
The defined steps in the process are defined as follows:

1. **Determining risk tolerance**: WealthNavi assesses each individual customer's risk tolerance based on factors such as his or her age and annual income, wealth accumulation objectives, target investment period, and planned monthly contributions. If customers' plans later change, they can update their target investment sizes and risk tolerance levels accordingly.
2. **Preparing an optimized portfolio**: WealthNavi prepares portfolios optimized for a customer's risk tolerance level. Investments are diversified among more than 10,000 companies in 50 countries via 6–7 exchange traded funds (ETFs).
3. **Accepting deposits:** Our investors can deposit funds through our partner SBI Sumishin Net Bank and through three main Japanese banks–all in real time: 24 hours a day, 365 days a year. Funds can also be transferred from other banks.
4. **Automating orders:** Our system links customers' PCs and smartphones to the New York Stock Exchange. As a rule, if funds are deposited by 8:00 p.m., orders for the various ETFs that make up the customer's ideal portfolio are automatically placed the following morning.
5. **Automatic reinvesting:** Unless otherwise specified by the customer, the system reinvests dividends automatically, in order to maximize the compounding interest effect that comes from long-term investing.
6. **Recurring investments**: It is also possible to set up regular automatic transfers from a saving account. As money is added, our patented system checks the customer's portfolio and orders are automatically placed to correct any deviations from the ideal portfolio.
7. **Automated rebalancing:** Twice a year, the portfolio is automatically rebalanced to account for any deviations that may have transpired due to market movements.
8. **Automated tax optimization**: Taxes on dividends or gains earned during rebalancing are carried forward to the following year by realizing any appropriate capital losses that have accrued on the ETFs that make up the portfolio.

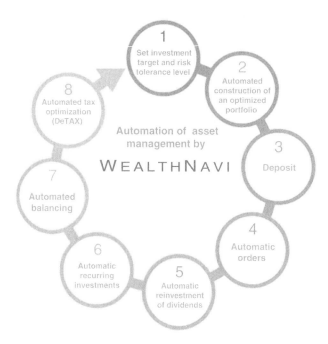

FIGURE 4.1 WealthNavi's Automated Asset Management
Source: WealthNavi.

Taking the Subjectivity out of Asset Management

KS: Services such as WealthNavi that provide computer-based automated asset management are referred to as robo-advisors. In the United States, their use has quickly spread, particularly among young people.

        We had been aware that the SBI Group had been interested in the potential of robo-advisors for some time. I have learned that among the various Japanese and overseas robo-advisors, the SBI Group chose to establish a partnership with WealthNavi because of our thorough objectivity, transparency, and technical know-how. Wealth-Navi is the only robo-advisor in Japan that has automated the entire process (as of December 2016) from target setting to tax optimization. It can be argued that this is a sign of the technical expertise of WealthNavi, where more than half of the employees are engineers. Our securities trading system was built on Amazon Web Service (AWS), making it the first such public use of this service in Japan.

        The company is also the first one in Japan to disclose its asset management algorithm, making independent verification possible. Furthermore, when choosing ETFs to form the portfolio, the best ones are selected using objective criteria–such as net assets and liquidity-expense ratio (all as part of our fiduciary pledge to place our customers' best interests first). WealthNavi is primarily used by busy working-age people, and 92% of users are aged 20–59 (as of August 2017). Since our official release in July 2016, 70,000 people have signed up for the service, and more than 60 billion yen has been deposited. This makes us the number-one robo-advisor in Japan.

Bringing the Bank-Brokerage-Robo–Advisor Model to Japan

KS: In October 2016, WealthNavi established a business partnership with SBI SECURITIES and SBI Sumishin Net Bank. Together, we are working to create a new business model that unites banks, securities companies, and robo-advisors. Clients of SBI SECURITIES and SBI Sumishin Net Bank can use WealthNavi by linking their accounts and enjoy integrated management of not only their deposits foreign-currency balances, stocks, and investment trust holdings but also financial assets managed via a robo-advisor. There are also plans to tie this to a smartphone app.

Unlike in the United States, in Japan, deposits are the main type of financial asset. As a result, a bank-brokerage–robo-advisor model is probably the key to accelerating the shift from savings to investments, as well as to providing complete asset management support for clients. Working with the SBI Group, we will take the lead in developing the bank-brokerage–robo-advisor model, and provide support for introducing the model to regional financial institutions.

Appealing to a Younger Generation through Micro-Investing

KS: In May 2017, WealthNavi and SBI Sumishin Net Bank jointly launched the micro-investment service Mametasu, the first such service in Japan. As an example of how it works, a user who makes a purchase of 420 yen at a convenience store using a credit card or digital wallet (such as Apple Pay) is able to round up the payment to 500 yen and invest the 80 yen in change.

This small amount of change is invested in a diversified portfolio of more than 11,000 companies in 50 countries through the WealthNavi platform. A banking API under development by SBI Sumishin Net Bank makes this micro-investment service possible. Achieving small-scale investment by combining the cutting-edge technology of the SBI Group and a FinTech startup is a prime example of effective, open innovation.

The spread of Apple Pay–which was introduced into Japan in October 2016–is accelerating the switch from paying with cash to paying with smartphones. Under these conditions, an app that makes it possible to make bit-by-bit investments with every smartphone purchase will probably make investing more familiar to a larger portion of the population, particularly young people. Going forward, WealthNavi plans to introduce the service to regional financial institutions as a powerful way to appeal to the younger demographic.

Fixing the Wealth Gap

KS: The Chinese classic Guanzi contains this passage: "When the granaries are full, [the people] will know propriety and moderation. When their clothing and food is adequate, they will know the distinction between honor and shame." Of course, it would be ideal if everyone valued learning over wealth like Confucian disciple Yan Hui[1], but one truth of human society is that having enough financial security to live without worry is a major contributor to individuals' peace of mind and tolerance within society.

The company's name WealthNavi–a combination of the words *wealth* and *navi*, short for *navigation*–invokes the image of a signpost to wealth. As people recognize that the growing wealth gap is problem in society, WealthNavi's use of FinTech to give anyone access to asset-management services previously only enjoyed by the wealthy is a potential cure for the economically stratified society and meets the needs of our time.

WealthNavi's Future Outlook

KS: There are a number of Asian countries that are currently experiencing strong economic growth, giving rise to a greater and greater need for asset management services. In partnership with the SBI Group–which was quick to promote investments in and partnerships with banks and securities companies

---

[1] Yan Hui was praised as the disciple of Confucius who loved learning the most, but who died young and impoverished, wanting neither government work nor social advancement. When Yan Hui died, Confucius lamented, "Alas! Heaven has forsaken me!" *Analects of Confucius*, Upper Text.

in Asian countries including Korea, Indonesia, Thailand, and Vietnam – we would like to introduce WealthNavi's robo-advisor service to the rapidly expanding middle class in these growing Asian economies.

In Japan, there are numerous successful FinTech startups, but there are few that possess both the status of a financial institution and the development skills of a tech company. With this special combination, we will continue working to develop and launch services that will help us succeed both in Japan and throughout Asia.

Automated Household Account Book and Cloud Accounting

Money Forward
  Representative: Yosuke Tsuji, Director and CEO
  Company profile
    Founded: 2012
    Number of customers: 5 million users (PFM)
    Partner companies: Shizuoka Bank, SBI Sumishin Net Bank, Mizuho Financial Group, Seven Bank, Yamaguchi Financial Group, and so on
  Having adopted a mission of "Money Forward. Move your life forward," Money Forward has two businesses – Money Forward, an automated household account book and asset management service, and MF Cloud Series, a cloud service for businesses.

Yoshitaka Kitao: Tell us about the history of the company.
Yosuke Tsuji: Money Forward was founded primarily through the efforts of Yosuke Tsuji, who previously worked at Monex, Toshio Taki, formerly of Nomura Securities, and Director Chihiro Asano, who developed the company's financial services. These members come from the financial industry and share the desire to solve financial problems though the power of technology. Although money is important for various life events, including marriage, the birth of a child, studying abroad, and old age, there is now an extremely limited number of opportunities for average Japanese citizens to study and learn about money. We launched our business to contribute to the creation of a society in which individual members have fewer concerns and worries about money, and an environment in which society possesses more vigor, so that they can become challenging because of changes to the flow of funds in Japan.

Automated Household Account Book and Asset Management Service Money Forward

YK: Tell us about your business.

YT: We introduced the automated household account book and asset management service, Money Forward, with a target market of individuals in Japan. This service collects usage information on more than 2,600 finance-related services, including banking, credit cards, securities, electronic money, shopping by mail, and account balances. We transform this information into a household account book. Our service is unique in that it automatically acquires, categorizes and graphs data from linked accounts. Purchased items and store names are automatically reflected in the household account book by having the user photograph receipts.

MF Cloud Series, Cloud Services for Businesses

YT: The cloud service MF Cloud Series[2] for businesses targets individual business owners and companies, and it charges a monthly or annual fee. MF Cloud Accounting, which automatically acquires the transaction details from more than 3,600 finance-related services, and automates journaling necessary for accounting operations, is a cloud-based software that can increase the efficiency of accounting operations and improve productivity. Furthermore, its automated accounting book includes such features as sales and expenses graphs. This makes it possible to ascertain business conditions in real time, whenever and wherever, via smartphone.

YK: What are the distinguishing features of the business environment?

YT: Until now, our growth has been centered on core technologies related to account aggregation and management, data analysis, and security. These core technologies by themselves are no more than functions that form the infrastructure to generate financial data,

---

[2] This refers to the following eight services: Income tax return software MF Cloud Income Tax Return, accounting software MF Cloud Accounting, invoice management software MF Cloud Billing, salary calculation software MF Cloud Salary, accounts receivable cash application software MF Cloud Accounts Receivable Cash Application, management software MF Cloud My Number, expense adjustment software MF Cloud Expenses, and fundraising service MF Cloud Finance.

but applications such as household account book and accounting software can show the value of using that data. Furthermore, these technologies create increase in functionality when tied to the services provided by various players.

Our first application, Money Forward, an automated household account book and asset management service, was released in December 2012, as catalyzed by expanding use of smartphones. Until then, we had provided various services that made use of account applications, but their use was limited to people who possessed a relatively high level of financial literacy because they were introduced as services for computers.

We were able to quickly launch a service that is geared toward smartphones, which resulted in its extensive use, and the service is growing into one that has captured the top market share in Japan.

In November 2013, we released MF Cloud Accounting/Income Tax Return, cloud-based accounting software. The service, which began as a response to demand among household account book users for software to handle tax returns for business income, was developed for people in jobs that require certification, such as accountants and tax accountants. It is widely used in the accounting operations of small- and medium-sized enterprises, at the dawn of cloud accounting software.

In Japan, tax accountants are indispensable, particularly for small- and medium-sized enterprises. Money Forward has drawn attention as a supporting service that dramatically increases operational efficiency through automation, and ease-of-use for field professionals.

These services are now used to handle the data of numerous individuals and corporations. In the context of FinTech, focus has fallen on the value of providing advice based on this information. We are seeking to build on these developments by increasing the understanding of financial institution clients and expanding user convenience through operational and capital tie-ups.

YK: Tell us about your actual growth.
YT: Money Forward has captured more than 5 million users over the years since its December 2012 launch. The service has won the top share of the market for household account book apps and boasts a satisfaction level of greater than 90%. In 2015, it was rated the top product in the free finance category on Apple's App Store, and on

Google Play it was selected as the best app in 2014 and 2015, and in 2016 for best local app.[3]

YK: Tell us how the business is progressing.
YT: I will provide some examples of use of the automated household account book and asset management service Money Forward.

1. A single man in his thirties who works at a financial company:
   - This individual experiences dramatic divergences across the size of different expenditures, and he increased the quality of his life by managing his household finances in such a way as to meet his necessities, while contemporaneously budgeting for his larger expenditures.
   - Because Money Forward enables him to check balances and receive transaction notifications for new deposits in real time, he has naturally become aware of these even during regular shopping.
   - The benefits of enhanced financial control have enabled him to accumulate 3 million yen in assets since starting use of the service.
2. A married man in his forties who works at an information service provider:
   - Upon being introduced to Money Forward, he was most impressed by the ease of entering information data related to credit card usage and bank withdrawals is automatically entered.
   - His wife is frugal and tends to economize, but after their assets became visible, she noticed that they had spare money and learned to enjoy various activities such as a certain amount of shopping at no sacrifice to her sense of financial security.
   - With Money Forward in place as an asset planning tool, he now feels that he can grow old with peace of mind.
3. A single female in her twenties who works at an IT company:
   - Until she started using Money Forward, she could not effectively control her spending impulses and she spent too much money, but she has now acquired the habit of managing her household finances in a disciplined manner.
   - She has been able to sustain this discipline, because the hassle of entering information was eliminated by linking the service to her bank and credit card.
   - With visible access to her balances, and by checking them daily (as she does her weight), she has eliminated wasteful spending.

---

[3] Internet survey conducted by Macromill Inc. (research company, Macromill Inc.; survey method, Internet survey; survey period, February 5–6, 2016; target, users of household account book apps in their 30s and 40s).

Expanding Money Forward to Financial Institutions

YK: Tell us about partnerships and collaborations with financial institutions.

YT: We provide an automated household account book and asset management service that is based on Money Forward, but includes expanded functions for the various financial institutional users. The basic functions are the same as those of Money Forward, but the service also makes it possible to post ads in a dedicated banner ad section.

Furthermore, the system provides added value, including the ability to send messages about special campaigns from financial institutions. We have introduced the service to 10 financial institutions (SBI Sumishin Net Bank, Yamaguchi Financial Group, Shizuoka Bank, Tokai Tokyo Securities, Toho Bank, Shiga Bank, The Gunma Bank, Fukui Bank, Okazaki Shinkin Bank, and Michinoku Bank).

Launch of Official Account: A Private Page for Financial Institutions

YT: Official Account is a private page for each financial institution, which can be created for the automated household account book and asset management service Money Forward app. It is displayed to users who link their savings account at the financial institution to the service. The private page offers customizable functions, such as a notification timeline document warehouse, and a direct link function that makes it possible to draw people to apps and websites provided by financial institutions. Introduced in 2016, about 30 firms, including banks and securities companies, now take part in the planning of the service.

Promotion of the Open Bank API Project

YT: This is a system that makes it possible, with the consent of the bank and customer, to use customer information gathered by banks (e.g., asset balance and deposit and withdrawal histories), for nonbank services, without the need to provide Internet banking login IDs and passwords to the nonbanking service (Figure 4.2). This enables access to accurate and secure data for nonbanking services at a low cost. In the IT industry, data use is being standardized, and banks themselves are becoming the platform for FinTech services. This is a cutting-edge effort even when compared to other countries, even overseas, as only a couple of banks are making such efforts.

Fundraising Service MF Cloud Finance

Money Forward announced the development of its fundraising service MF Cloud Finance in partnership with 10 financial institutions.
A new credit model using account data was built.

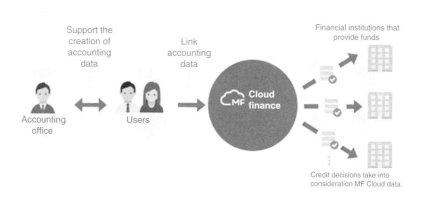

FIGURE 4.2 MF Cloud Finance
Source: Money Forward material (released April 2016).

Making Use of the Fund-Raising Service MF Cloud Finance

YT: MF Cloud Series users can raise funds from financial institutions using data from the cloud accounting software MF Cloud Accounting/Income Tax Return and invoice management software MF Cloud Billing. Because this eliminates the need to prepare documents, it is possible to expedite and facilitate the capital raising process. Our first initiative in this area was the listing of financing products provided by GMO Epsilon (January 2017).

Shift from Data Aggregation to Problem Solutions

YK: Tell us what you will focus on in the future.

YT: It has been four years since introducing the service, and we have had certain successes regarding the analysis of past and present financial conditions of individuals and corporations. In addition, through partnerships with financial institutions and policy proposals, we are creating a model to use information that involves financial institutions providing APIs and users making appropriate use of their own data.

The added value we provide, however, is still biased toward aggregating and making information visible, and we have not reached the phase when we provide all of solutions that users actually want. Our mission is "Money Forward. Move your life forward." We would like to provide solutions to the money problems of users, and help both individuals and corporations live constructive lives through our technology and services.

Toward a Solution for Money Problems and Greater Productivity

YT: Over the next 10 years, as technology becomes more and more advanced, we would like to facilitate current trends toward a cashless society by 2020, and help provide answers to the two major issues that confront Japan: the declining birthrate and the growing percentage of the population that is elderly.

Japan will rapidly make progress toward eliminating the use of cash as 2020, the year that the Tokyo will host the Olympics and Paralympics, approaches. A world in which all financial transactions are conducted electronically, and a new type of accompanying information becomes available, will evolve. This will feature greater use of electronic money, more frequent use of credit cards, and use of electronic data interchange (EDI) for information accompanying remittances. For example, attaching information and functions when consumers receive customized coupons linked to past payment information, business invoices, salary information, and bank transfer information, will generate flows of money. These objectives will probably be achieved by banks and combinations of various service APIs.

Then, sometime in 2020 or later, it will finally become necessary to implement various responses to the graying (aging) of society, a problem that is growing more and more serious by the day. We argue that when the future of the pension and medical system is uncertain, it is necessary to provide an information infrastructure that helps address these issues so that young people can raise children and accumulate assets with peace of mind. We must also further evolve Money Forward as a tool for asset accumulation and the attendant security it provides by making full use of advice provided by artificial intelligence (AI).

In the field of business, there are growing concerns about a looming shortage of workers, particularly young ones. Japanese businesses have a labor productivity that is only 60% of that in the United States, and we would like to provide solutions to these problems, involving incremental productivity and decision-making efficiencies, in part through real-time business analysis.

In order to facilitate the creation of this type of society, we endeavor to promote the use of IT by individuals and companies, to provide solutions to money problems, and to increase the productivity of small- and medium-sized enterprises. We are doing so by capturing a greater market share for our individual services and working to resolve problems in partnership with people and companies who possess the same desire. As part of these efforts, we are moving forward with proposing finance- and IT-related policies through the in-house FinTech Lab, and we established the Business IT Promoters Association (BIPA) in October 2016.

We want to solve various problems that Japan is likely to face in the future, and to make a contribution to society by reducing the work and increasing the productivity of individuals and companies, for the benefit of individuals and society as a whole.

Savings App

infcurion group
  Representative: Hiroki Maruyama, Director
  Company profile
    Founded: 2006
    Number of customers, market share: handles largest volume among smartphone payment service providers (31.8% in 2014)
    Example of customers: NTT Docomo, SoftBank, Recruit, SBI Sumishin Net Bank
  The Infcurion Group operates two businesses: one that provides consulting services for payments in the financial field, and another that provides payment solutions. Its subsidiary NestEgg Inc. offers a savings app for individuals in Japan and is planning on expanding into Asia.

Yoshitaka Kitao: Tell us about the history of the company.
Hiroki Maruyama: In 1999, when the Internet was quickly spreading, electronic commerce (EC) and portal sites drew all the attention,

but I thought that payment services were the most evolved, so I contacted JCB about working together. JCB was involved in several new efforts, such as developing a model for using artificial intelligence (AI) to detect misconduct and undertaking marketing that employs payment data and launching new businesses. After that, in 2006, with a desire to generate innovation from a broader perspective than the existing framework, I established the Infcurion Group.

Following our launch, we expanded various businesses to promote a cashless society and FinTech, which included the mPOS business to spread payment infrastructure, a business that supports the launch of new payment-related systems, as well as the research and publishing businesses. A subsidiary, NestEgg Inc., was established in April 2016, and was organized to launch finbee, an automated savings app.

App for Natural Savings

YK: Tell us about your business.

HM: The automated saving app finbee was introduced to make financial services more familiar, and the company's work was based on the concept of "introducing savings into life." This business does not simply provide users with financial services, but tries to integrate these products into routine activities.

The company provides apps and Internet-based services that make it possible to naturally save during daily activities. For example, it is possible to set numerous automated savings rules, such as saving change from purchases, saving transit fares and gas by walking, allocating excess funds to savings, and so on. It is also possible to build up savings with others, including a spouse, friends, and so on. (Of course, information such as account balances and what savings are for is not shared due to privacy considerations.) This approach makes it possible to avoid the struggle to economize on one's own and, instead, allows people to save money while enjoying themselves, communicating with others, and working toward what one desires.

In other words, this service can even be used by people who, under previous living modes, have not been able to accumulate assets or save, no matter what they do. People find it difficult, in general, to continue activities that they are not emotionally tied to in daily life, such as working toward future benefits. Therefore, our service makes it possible to build up a comfort level with the concept of savings and to create the foundation for investing and building assets for the future, by first saving for something that one wants in the near future.

A Business Model That Does Not Rely on User Fees

HM: This service is targeted to consumers who are not typically charged a usage fee. Revenue is generated by introducing and sending users to stores that can capture purchases made with the saved money, and conducting joint marketing with financial institutions.

We use data to project individual purchases a couple of months into the future instead of forecasts of consumer behavior, which also makes this a revolutionary new advertising business model.

YK: Tell us about the business environment.

HM: One of the issues that we face is that of the cash-based society. In Japan, an extremely large percentage of people have bank accounts and credit cards, but less than 20% of people make use of Internet banking or electronic payments. In other words, although it appears that there are extensive financial services in the country, IT-based financial services have not taken hold to the extent that they have in other countries (Figure 4.3).

This pattern has persisted despite many companies and organizations having promoted Internet banking and credit cards, suggesting that a new approach is required. As such, we decided to focus on user-centered smartphones and to provide services that are extensions of daily living, not financial services.

There was, however, the initial issue of where money would be saved. For example, we even examined methods such as using the savings to charge prepaid cards, but thought that it would be a problem if the savings could not be repaid for some reason, and that Japanese consumers are psychologically predisposed against placing large sums of money into entities other than financial institutions. While we continued to examine if various ideas, such as saving money by linking to banks, were possible, financial institutions began releasing APIs.

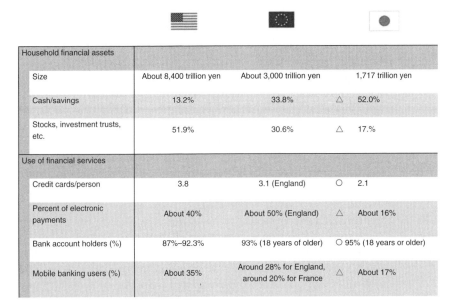

	🇺🇸	🇪🇺		🇯🇵
Household financial assets				
Size	About 8,400 trillion yen	About 3,000 trillion yen		1,717 trillion yen
Cash/savings	13.2%	33.8%	△	52.0%
Stocks, investment trusts, etc.	51.9%	30.6%	△	17.%
Use of financial services				
Credit cards/person	3.8	3.1 (England)	○	2.1
Percent of electronic payments	About 40%	About 50% (England)	△	About 16%
Bank account holders (%)	87%–92.3%	93% (18 years of older)	○	95% (18 years or older)
Mobile banking users (%)	About 35%	Around 28% for England, around 20% for France	△	About 17%

FIGURE 4.3 Comparison of Financial Service Use in Various Countries
Source: Material created by infcurion using "Flow of Funds Comparison" for Japan, United States, and Europe, issued by the Bank of Japan and "Whitepaper Information and Communications" in Japan, released by the Ministry of Internal Affairs and Communications.

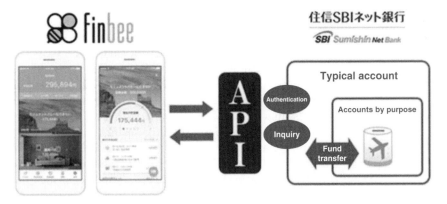

FIGURE 4.4 Partnership between finbee and SBI Sumishin Net Bank
Source: SBI Sumishin Net Bank press release.

In other words, the introduction of bank APIs was the major catalyst for launching this business. Money that is automatically saved is deposited in the user's bank account, and it never passes through our hands. We instruct the financial institution to deposit the money via an API.

I also serve as the representative director of the FinTech Association Japan and feel every day that many entities, including financial institutions and related government agencies, have begun to recognize the importance of open innovation and the API economy. Our service is possible precisely because of this environment, in which FinTech is not simply a buzzword but a driving force for major change.

YK: Tell us about the response of customers.
HM: The results of a consumer survey reveal that 90% of respondents are aware that savings is an issue, and most of them rate finbee highly. For example, even users that save a set amount each month are able to flexibly use our service to do so in a manner that is appropriate for their monthly household income and expenses, and some users even enjoy seeing the amount that they save automatically.

One user who could not save no matter what he tried commented that he would be able to save if it were automatic, and that he would continue to do so if he were saving with another party.

YK: Tell us about partnerships and collaborations with financial institutions.
HM: Our service was launched through a partnership with SBI Sumishin Net Bank (Figure 4.4). When the announcement was made, various financial institutions inquired about the service because it was the first case of an update-type API, and there were benefits for the retail business of financial institutions. In particular, these include capturing active accounts, increasing card use fees, providing financing in the case of insufficient funds for a particular purpose, investing and managing excess funds, and proposing financial instruments for life events determined to be the purpose of the savings.

In light of this, we are moving forward with an examination of partnerships with numerous financial institutions. Our service is often given as a good example of open innovation, especially during discussions with the central bank and related agencies.

In addition, when we were making the initial proposal to financial institutions, there were many that requested a finbee function be added to their portal app.

That would, of course, be useful for customers who are frequent users of a particular bank. However, for users whom financial institutions have yet to reach (customers who do not have an account or use the service, young people, etc.) developing our app in accordance with how users live their lives, not with financial services in mind, is the most appropriate pathway. After explaining this concept, the vast majority of financial institutions wanted to use finbee because it was not simply used as a link into their portal app. Furthermore, some financial institutions want both—not only to include the software in their portal app, but also to simply and directly connect to our app—and are endeavoring to develop an approach in different markets.

In addition to inquiries about partnerships regarding savings accounts from banks and credit unions, we received outreach from securities companies, and we moved forward with examining tie-ups that link users who had accumulated savings, little by little, to investment opportunities.

Connecting Life Information and Finance

YK: Tell us what you will focus on in the future.

HM: We will expand our partnerships with financial institutions, so that mapped savings will flow to even more of these entities. Furthermore, we will create API links with companies that provide content and services related to desired goods and activities, and connect life information to finance through API functions.

We also plan to connect to various services through APIs, such as savings tied to income other than salary, by expanding customer-to-customer (C2C) marketplace, sharing, and so on. Beyond this, we are seeking to facilitate savings based on cryptocurrencies and points, and to promote household finance management and investment.

Efforts will also be made to evolve proposals and behavior forecasts using AI analysis. With general data analysis, we analyze results information (e.g., ad views). Our algorithms are designed to project what people want to buy in the future, target period, and existing savings balances. This makes it possible to develop more precise proposals related to behavior forecasts and recommendations.

It is said that these services are geared for the Japanese, but we are conducting a detailed examination of the possibility of introducing them across Asia. Of course, Japan has a different culture and environment, but our objective is to provide a service indispensable for users, as society changes to one in which there are greater consumption and activities within a cash-based society, similar to Japan.

A Savings App as an Introduction to Financial Services

HM: In Japan, the objective is to expand the use of savings apps such as ours until they are used in a manner similar to credit and ATM cards. Furthermore, our goal is to create a transforming "neo bank," with the hook of offering all financial services, not simply savings.

For example, if electronic payments used to save change from purchases take root in daily life, the percentage of private final consumption paid for via electronic payments will increase to at least 50%, which is comparable to that in Europe and the United States. It would be wonderful if various objectives could be achieved, such as having investments account for more than 50% of the household financial products undertaken by consumers who have gained experience through saving. We are also striving to spread our service as a new ad media market.

YK: What should finance look like in 10 years?

HM: Across the next decade, it will probably be necessary for the industry to maintain or accelerate its rate of change. It would be desirable to create an ecosystem so that finance can continue to evolve as society undergoes major changes, such as the development of AI and integration with the Internet of Things (IoT).

There is, therefore, a need to switch the exchange of financial data and payments to electronic format, and this switch should involve almost zero costs. Blockchains are probably one way to achieve this, and various advances are necessary, including direct payment methods that make use of APIs.

In 10 years, useres' financial knowledge and IT literacy will be substantially greater than what it is today. If users can obtain all types of information and access financial services when they want, financial products and financial regulation will probably no longer be the exclusive domain of the central government.

That is, users should be the rule markers and finance should become more democratic, which is what we are working to realize.

Crowdfunding

Music Securities Inc.
    Representative: Masami Komatsu, Director
    Company profile
        Founded: 2001
        Number of customers: 69 companies (partner financial institutions)
        Partners: Shiga Bank, 77 Bank, Kumamoto Prefecture, and others

Music Securities operates the investment crowdfunding platform Securite, which connects businesses to individuals, and allows users to collect money and social media contacts and friends. In partnership with financial institutions and local governments, the company has experience managing funds that have raised more than 7.0 billion yen.

Yoshitaka Kitao: Tell us about the history of the company.

Masami Komatsu: I was a musician when I was a student. It takes money to make music. At that time, the only way to acquire funds was to associate with a major record label or music agent. If a record company provides funding, the musician needs to make music the record company, not the musician, wants. If the record companies take all the risk, they have all the rights. At that time, I learned the very important and obvious point that without economic independence, there is no creative independence.

With the desire to create a financial institution providing economic independence for musicians, I established Music Securities Inc. in 2000. I quickly created a music fund through an anonymous partnership. It was a small fund that raised only 860 thousand yen. I created the contracts by scratch, signed artists, negotiated with investors, created CDs, and marketed and promoted them, which resulted in a return of 13.31%. It was a small first step but a critical one in taking us to where we are now.

After that, I developed the Securite investment fund, which is not limited to music. I have created more than 620 funds in various business fields.

Investment Crowd Financing That Is Not Simply Fundraising

YK: Tell us about your business.

MK: Our business is based on a new Financial Instruments and Exchange Act–compliant financing system for soliciting funds from individual investors over the Internet and then distributing a certain percentage of the revenue from the business to investors.

For business operators, this is a new method for raising funds, and for investors, the platform provides new investment opportunities. The business model is based on intermediating between the two parties as a type II financial instruments business operator registered with the Financial Services Agency. Securite is not simply the name of the service, but an Internet-based investment platform that integrates various functions, including payments investor and fund management (through individual pages for each investor), IR systems, mail magazines and blog systems, and a due diligence system.

We generate revenues by charging a fee to both investors and business operators. Recently, this approach has generally come to be referred to as *investment crowd funding*. Our focus involves implementing a business plan that effectively deploys the capital that is raised. It does not end with the funding cycle itself.

Investors pay on average 8% of the amount committed as a sales fee. (See the arrow marked [1] in Figure 4.5) For example, if 10,000 yen is invested, we take 800 yen as our fee from the 10,800 paid, and then provide the business operator with 10,000 yen.

Support for Business Plans and Audits

MK: Business operators pay a fixed, upfront fee regardless of the amount of funds to be raised. (See the arrow marked [2] in Figure 4.5.) We use that money to create web content to solicit investors and cover the cost of accountants required for audits, and attorneys for legal reviews.

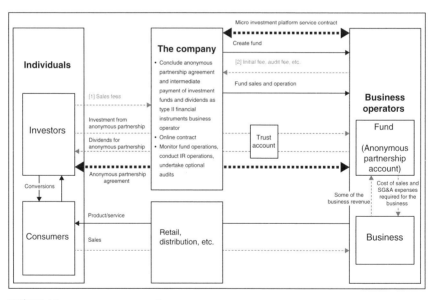

FIGURE 4.5 Investment Crowd Financing
Source: Music Securities.

If necessary, we also provide support for the formulation of a business plan. The amount of the initial fee depends on the amount of work involved.

Furthermore, business operators undergo a voluntary audit by our company's certified public accountant once a year. Information from the audit is disclosed to investors. The audit expense is about 100,000 yen annually.

We charge a system-use fee for implementing product promotions via our investor-only mail magazine and individual pages for investor and IR activities using a smartphone app. Additionally, we assess an administration fee of 1%–2% of the total amount of money raised for the fund, which is used to cover various expenses, including the cost of creating the investment trust.

Shift from a Focus on Collateral to Business Feasibility

YK: What are the distinguishing features of the business environment?

MK: There have been major changes in the business environment on two fronts. First, greater importance is being placed on business feasibility during the financing screening, because of changes in the Financial Services Agency's guidelines for supervision of financial institutions. This is a shift away from the traditional emphasis on collateral to financing based on evaluation of future business plans.

Many regional financial institutions are interested in our anonymous partnership funds because of this feature. During the screening to create a fund, the greatest emphasis is placed on the certainty of the future business plan. This method, which makes it possible to supply funds taking into consideration the results of the screening, leads to the provision of funds based on evaluation of the business feasibility. Working with us, many regional financial institutions have come to provide business capital on this basis. We are now creating business tie-ups with financial institutions throughout Japan.

Hopes for Revitalizing Local Communities and Growth Money

MK: The second business shift is the urgent, pressing need to revitalize local communities. One of the many challenges here is the lack of capital-like funds for small- and medium-sized entities that operate in these communities – that is, growth money for risk-taking initiatives.

Business operators primarily raise funds through loans from financial institutions. Startup companies endeavoring to go public can also raise funds through a third-party allotment of shares. Even so, many local business operators find it difficult to raise additional funds from financial institutions, or to obtain funding from venture capital companies. There are hopes, therefore, that raising risk money using our system will be a third form of financial intermediation. Without risk capital, it would probably be difficult for companies to grow and employment to increase, because entrepreneurs would not have sufficient resources to take on the challenge of creating new businesses.

In addition, the Cabinet Office (see www.cao.go.jp/index-e.html) spread investment crowdfunding systems among local governments in order to promote their use in communities throughout Japan. These efforts included the Furusato Investment Liaison Conference. The Financial Services Agency also holds the Risk Money Supply Promotion Forum throughout Japan and we announced the investment crowdfunding system compliant with the Financial Instruments and Exchange Act across the country.

Owing to these efforts by the central government to spread such activities, there has been an increase in local government measures to supply growth money. We are undertaking joint work with or have been commissioned by about 30 local (prefectural and municipal) governments, and are now playing a role in raising money for various regions. In particular, for many of the funds, investments from nonregional entities account for more than 70% of the total funds raised. We have established an "inflow of growth money," and created a successful model for regional revitalization measures.

YK: Tell us how the business is progressing.

MK: We measure the success of our business by how many more enterprises for which we can provide funding, and the number of funds we operate. Between the fiscal year ending March 2012 and the fiscal year ending March 2016, the number of funds has grown fivefold – from 56 to 272.

Another indicator is the number of financial institutions with which we have partnered. We are creating a business ecosystem (Securite-Local Bank-Ecosystem) that makes it possible for business operators throughout Japan who need funds to meet each other: a fee-based business matching service. This work started with our tie-up with Shiga Bank in 2010, and we have now created partnerships with 69 financial institutions. Through this ecosystem, we conduct business matching for about 150 companies a month.

YK: Tell us about your clients and business partners.

MK: We are being introduced to financial institutions that have fundraising needs through the previously discussed Security-Local

Bank-Ecosystem. We also interact with business operators who want to connect with individual investors, not simply to meet short-term funding needs, through Securite. In addition, we promote the use of Securite as a sales tool for financial institutions targeting businesses with which they do not have existing relationships.

After the introduction, we hold meetings with all business operators. Here, we explain our approach, including the nature of the funds to be raised, the need to rework business plans, the importance of IR, the handling of dividends, and our fee structure. When we conclude an agreement (see line marked micro-investing platform service agreement in Figure 4.5) with the business operator, we begin to screen the business. After the screening process is complete, we create a fund and solicit contributions from investors through Securite. Then, 10%–30% of the initial fee paid by the business operator is passed on to investors as a business matching fee.

We are also moving forward with fund sales collaborations through Securite-Local Bank-Ecosystem. Here, we will link Securite with the websites of four regional financial institutions, and increase our points of contact with investors. Furthermore, for the Yamaguchi Prefecture–based Saikyo Bank, we developed an API link between the bank's Internet banking system and the Securite system, and the bank sells our funds just like it does other financial products.

It is also possible to do the same with various banks by joining the Securite-LocalBank-Ecosystem, and notifying the local Finance Bureau of the changes in sales of financial products. For Internet banking, we would like to increase the number of API links related to the sales of our funds in the future.

YK: Tell us some actual examples.

MK: Funds raised through crowdfunding based on an anonymous partnership agreement can be considered loan capital if certain conditions are met. In other words, when financial institutions conduct lending screening, funds that are usually recorded as loans under liabilities are recognized as good capital. A growing number of funds are being formed using this approach. For financial institutions, this makes it possible to upgrade the borrower category, increase lending and reduce allowances.

I would like to discuss an example of a fund for a manufacturing business operator. The company was in poor financial condition, making it difficult to obtain additional loans, but it had reworked its future business plan. The fund was created on the condition that the funds would be a capital loan, and because the funds were viewed as capital, the company could receive additional lending from regional banks, make capital investments for its factory and increase sales.

Furthermore, when the great East Japan earthquake hit, we introduced a series of investment products called Securite victim support funds. A model example is the fund for Yagisawa Shoten located in the city of Rikuzentakada-shi, Iwate. Established in 1807, Yagisawa Shoten is a soy sauce manufacturer with a history that dates back more than 200 years. We created two funds for them (one for 100 million yen and one for 50 million yen) for a total of 150 million yen, and more than 4,248 people invested in the funds. The fund raised the largest amount of money through crowd funding up to that time, and the money that was raised was used to rebuild the factory. The company was also able to capture customers because the 4,284 investors were stakeholders. Many people expressed the belief that the presence of the fund created a support community, and this became a driving force to rebuild the business. This is a crowdfunding mechanism that makes use of FinTech, but it is also a method for investing with a visible face that connects people to people.

Reducing the Time Required to Raise Funds

YK: Tell us what you will focus on in the future.

MK: The environment in which small- and medium-sized startup companies operate is undergoing major changes, including the migration of corporate information to cloud-based platforms. In particular, cloud accounting and financial software are capturing a larger share of the market, and vast amounts of data are being moved to the cloud.

We are moving forward with efforts to make use of this data by creating an API link that connects to the Securite system. The first example of this was the decision to form a business tie-up with Money Forward Inc. This made it possible to dramatically reduce the amount of time it takes to collect material required for screening. Furthermore, we receive requests to create funds from not only business operators but also from accounting offices that support those businesses. It is also possible to quickly disseminate IR information from the cloud by linking APIs to investor management databases. The business scheme is not changing, but FinTech is being used in a wider and wider range of fields.

Supplying Funds from Japan to Abroad

MK: Another important objective is the overseas expansion. Our company is creating numerous funds that make it possible for Japanese investors to invest in overseas businesses. For example, in 2009, we launched a fund for microfinancing for Cambodia and Indonesia. In addition, through a partnership established in 2014 with development banks in the United States and Europe, we created a financial institution fund that provides financing for small farmers in Peru.

In countries throughout the world, businesses are targeting Japan as a source of direct investment capital, and because of this, we responded by developing a business model to capture this opportunity. Using an approach based on Japan-style anonymous partnerships, we seek to introduce a mechanism for investors in countries other than Japan to invest in businesses in that country. In expanding overseas, we will establish joint ventures with local partners and create a cross-border system so that investors in that country can invest in Japanese businesses.

Our 10-year goal is to raise more than 100 billion yen annually from individual investors, an amount equivalent to the current aggregate value of Japanese venture investment. Once we achieve that objective, it may be possible to argue that anonymous partnerships are a new and innovative form of financial intermediation.

If we reach our target investment levels, it will also promote industry in the regions where the capital is allocated. In these jurisdictions, it can be expected that more businesses will be created by young people, the number of managers willing embrace the challenge of taking over a business – including the liabilities of the predecessor will increase, and more artists will be in a position to create music that they want.

In a hundred years, the financial industry will be dramatically different and there will be different players, and FinTech will accelerate these changes several-fold. I can feel that such an era is approaching. We will do all we can to be a change agent in this area.

Payments

BASE
  Representative: Yuta Tsuruoka, Director and CEO
  Company profile
  Founded: 2012

Customers: about 400,000 (merchants)

Partners: Sumitomo Mitsui Card, Sony Payment Services

With a mission of "simplifying the exchange of value and making it possible for people throughout the world to undertake optimal economic activities," BASE develops and introduces e-commerce platforms and online payment services that simplify payments.

Yoshitaka Kitao: Tell us about the history of the company.

Yuta Tsuruoka: Working with entrepreneur Kazuma Ieiri, I have created several Internet service enterprises. Having built businesses with little thought that nonetheless generated a response among many people, we felt the power and wonder of the technology referred to as the Internet, so we applied ourselves to the expansion of useful consumer services.

At that time, we launched the online shop development service BASE project because of something simple my mother said (more to follow). BASE service started as a project, but one month later, it was transformed into a corporation, BASE Inc.

Formidable Obstacles to Creating an E-Commerce Business

YT: In 1995, Windows 95 computers, which came equipped with a function to connect to the Internet as a standard feature, went on sale, and it was said that a period of Internet-based sales had arrived. However, programming and web design skills were required, and it was not easy for people to conduct sales on a routine basis over the Internet.

In order to conduct e-commerce (EC), a certain amount of knowledge of IT was required and people had to either spend time to acquire that knowledge through study or spend money to outsource the work to companies or people who possessed those skills. People needed to invest in technology, dedicating time and large amounts of money to conduct EC. This did not change for some time.

The concept of BASE was born in the spring of 2012. My mother, who ran a women's clothing retail store in a shopping district in Oita, said that she wanted to launch an online shop. At that time, there were several EC services provided by major companies. At first, I recommended those services to my mother, but when I looked at their details, I discovered that it would be difficult for my mother, who was in her fifties, to operate them. Additionally, the high cost to launch was also a formidable obstacle, making it ultimately impossible for my mother to open the shop. There were no tools for ordinary people like my mother to easily conduct EC.

Shift from Platform to Payment Services

YT: Because of my mother's comment, I started to form the idea of BASE, which would make it possible for anyone to easily create an online shop for free. Since I lived in a shared house at that time, I started to develop the services with the help of an engineer who was my housemate, and then gradually attracted more and more people to the project. As efforts progressed, driven mainly by people who were born in the 1990s or after (including me), we ran up against the critical issue of payments.

The payment industry is very old, and its structure is complicated. As we researched issues for BASE, we noticed that there was an extremely large number of opportunities for payment industry optimization. Having become extremely interested in payments, I decided that the core of the BASE business would be taking on the challenge of upgrading the payment process technology. Since we were pioneers in this field, as well as a startup company, this was an extremely big challenge for us.

The results of our efforts have included the release of the products identified next.

EC Platform BASE

YK: Tell us about your business.
YT: We have positioned three services as our core businesses – the EC platform BASE (for creating online shops that includes a shopping app), the online payment service PAY.JP, and the ID-based payment service PAY ID.

BASE is an online shop-creation service used by individuals for the commercial distribution of their products, corporations that launch businesses, and government entities. Additionally, it is an EC platform that provides an app that makes it possible to purchase products from shops that have opened in a particular mall.

As of May 2015, about 400,000 stores were using BASE. Since this platform forms the infrastructure necessary for EC, including such features as easy-to-introduce payment functions, appealing design templates, and transaction analysis tools, it is easy for even people who struggle to launch operations to participate in EC.

BASE was initially launched as a consumer-to-consumer (C2C) service, and it was often covered in the media alongside flea-market apps, but in fact, it is positioned as a tool for small business-to-consumer (B2C) businesses. Many individuals and companies use it as a tool to launch and sell original brands.

Previously, C2C sales were primarily conducted via auctions, but about 2012, flea-market apps were introduced and C2C services drew greater attention. Just as is the case for flea-market apps, it is simple to introduce products with BASE, but BASE is a platform used by stores selling products they make, not reselling products. It is also a service that makes it possible for product enterprises to easily conduct EC, and that spreads the value of these products over the Internet.

BASE is perceived as an important tool for retail stores, many of which in fact make use of the service. However, virtually any type of enterprise, including small- and medium-sized sole proprietorships, businesses, and government entities, can sell all types of products on the platform. The service can handle a wide range of products – from items made by my mother – to signature products of major companies (Figure 4.6).

The shopping-mall app is provided as one part of the company's services for building a system to promote sales of products offered by shops opened using BASE.

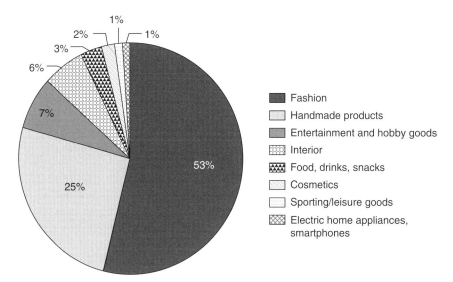

FIGURE 4.6 Breakdown by Category of Products Sold on BASE Shops
Source: BASE.

About one year after launching operations, we introduced the app, and in 2013, it was selected as the App Store's best app.

At that time, it was mainly used as a catalog to introduce products. In June 2015, it was updated as a shopping app with a payment feature that makes it easy to purchase products offered by participating stores, and it is now drawing the most attention as a service for BASE customers.

The app is available through both the App Store and Google Play. Users can search for items they like from those offered by the approximately 400,000 stores that use our online shop-creation service, ranging from fashion products to official goods of celebrities, plants, furniture, and home electronics. Furthermore, payments can be smoothly processed in as little as five seconds, if users sign up for PAY ID. As of October 2016, it was also compatible with Apple Pay.

Online Payment Service PAY.JP

YT: Introduced in September 2015, PAY.JP is a service for business operators and developers that makes it possible to easily, and at no charge, introduce credit card payment function to existing web services and EC sites. Although it is a B2B service, it can be used by individuals and companies. Because it resolves complex problems related to online payment services such as application time, cost, and ease of use, it is a very useful tool for Internet commerce and further invigorates business activities undertaken over the Internet. The service is compatible with six different credit cards (Visa, MasterCard, AMEX, JCB, Diners Club, and Discover Card), and is compliant with the PCIDSS international security standards.

ID-Based Payment Service PAY ID

YT: PAY ID makes it possible for purchasers to make online payments for web services and EC sites that have introduced PAY.JP, using a member ID and password. Multiple credit cards can be registered with PAY ID, so it is possible to use different ones for different purposes. At present, PAY ID payments can be used at about 400,000 participating merchants.

Both BASE and PAY.JP (PAY ID) are based on a payment fee model.

Limits to Making Use of Payment Proxy Services

YK: Tell us about changes in the business environment.

YT: BASE concluded an agreement with Sumitomo Mitsui Cards and
        Smart Link Network (currently SONY Payment Service) in 2014,
        and together we launched the independent payment system, BASE
        Simple Payment.

        In 2012, BASE was making use of PayPal for payments. In order
        to eliminate the burden on stores when introducing payment
        service, we arranged for the execution of a blanket contract and
        launched operations. At the time, we faced the major risk that it
        could become impossible to handle payments at all the stores if
        there were a problem at even one of the stores.

        PayPal raised the issue of the need for each store to execute an
        individual contract with the payment service provider, as opposed
        to the BASE blanket contract approach, this approach would force
        us to introduce a different method for payments.

        However, it was not very realistic for each store to enter into
        an agreement with the payment service provider. The process is a
        burdensome and time-consuming one and it runs contrary to the
        BASE service concept of making it easy for individuals to launch
        an online shop.

        BASE's goal is to enable users to make almost instantaneous
        payments until they are actually able to use the full range of our
        services. This could not be achieved using the services of existing
        payment service providers.

        At that time, we received proposals from several payment ser-
        vice providers, but most indicated that their processes, including
        screening, would take several weeks to complete. No one could
        provide us with a solution involving immediate service usage. We
        did not want to eliminate screening, but our ideal solution was to
        make it possible to access payment services instantaneously even
        if the same screening continued to be done.

        In fact, it was impossible to immediately have access to pay-
        ment services with existing screening methods, and this made our
        idea extremely difficult to execute upon at that time.

        Furthermore, because the cast of interested parties involved in
        payment services is extremely complicated, we could not reach our
        objectives on our own–and neither could payment service providers.

Creating Services through Business Tie-Ups

YT: At that time, we realized that it would be necessary to obtain the
        cooperation of acquirers (companies that manage participating

merchants) as well as payment service providers to realize BASE's objectives. We consulted with the various companies, and Smart Link Network (present-day SONY Payment Service) helped us with the type of payment service we wanted to create. We also started to look at partnerships with acquirers.

After about a year of negotiations, early in 2014, we announced a business tie-up with the acquirer Sumitomo Mitsui Card and with payment service provider Smart Link Network.

We then switched the payment function, which had previously been provided via PayPal, to our proprietary BASE Simple Payment, and launched the service. Simultaneously, we introduced escrow services (payment intermediation) to BASE.

When establishing business tie-ups, we stressed ensuring safety on BASE's side. For example, BASE serves as an intermediary, taking on the liability if buyers do not receive a product within a certain amount of time.

In addition, because it takes time to achieve compliance with security standards, we outsourced certain aspects of security to Smart Link Network. Doing so, it became possible to achieve instant screening when introducing payment services for newly opened online shops.

Moving toward the FinTech Era

YT: These efforts will increase convenience for stores. Before we introduced the service, billing statements sent to buyers only gave the name BASE, but since then, it has been possible to issue statements with the name of each store, and we have gradually built an environment in which users can use BASE as a full-service business platform.

In addition, it is possible to terminate use for individual stores that create problems, including those operated by anti-social forces or those conducting unlicensed sales, and we used these prerogatives to eliminate risks in our network.

Around the time we announced our entry into the payment business through PAY.JP on February 5, 2015, FinTech was already a field that was drawing attention overseas, particularly in the United States and Asia. In Japan, awareness was more limited. PAY.JP was launched in September 2015, and the situation changed at the beginning of 2016, when FinTech started to draw attention as a core economic opportunity.

Five years after establishing the company, we are expanding the scope of its businesses and winning awards from independent organizations. The attention that FinTech is drawing is generating a tailwind for us. Financial institutions are aggressively competing against one another, and I feel that the time has finally arrived for structural changes in the payment industry. But our mission to optimize payments is primarily driven by the factors other than the ebbs and flows and interest drawn by the field of FinTech. We expect to continue down the course we have set, ideally, decades into the future.

High Praise from Owners Who Know the Difficulty of EC

YK: Tell us how the business is progressing.
YT: The cumulative number of BASE shops that have opened is a prominent figure that indicates the company's growth. Each year since launch, we have more than doubled the number of shops on our platform. More than 10,000 new stores open every month now.

I will now discuss some of the high praise that the service has won from merchants that have introduced BASE. One established senbei (rice cracker) manufacturer introduced BASE for its EC operations when it launched its own brand in 2015.

Because the shop owner had a background related to web design, he understood the difficulty of launching the company's EC operations, and summarized our service in the following manner: "the fact that operating an online shop using BASE is not burdensome is extremely helpful for manufacturers." His company draws a lot of attention, as it has grown into a popular shop that receives requests for appearances from the media, and sells out of its products sold over the Internet.

Chat Support Regardless of the Size of the Company

YT: Progate Inc., which operates the online programming learning service "Progate," highly rated the ease of PAY.JP and support system both before and after introducing the service.

They chose PAY.JP for the following reason: "The documentation for developers is extremely simple. It had a detailed tutorial, and I was surprised that I could get a test fee system up and running in about ten minutes. . . . I thought that a fee system would be extremely bothersome and complicated, but when I realized that I could actually build a system myself, I thought that if that is true, even I could introduce the service" (comments given by Progate Inc. about PAY.JP).

Using the chat service Slack, PAY.JP provides prompt support for companies that have introduced the service. We received the following comment regarding this point: "I had no experience developing payment systems and was concerned about various aspects such as building the system and handling security. I was amazed at the quick response to inquiries for advice and requests from a small startup company like mine, and I think it is an extremely trustworthy service." The company launched the Progate fee-based plan without incident after introducing PAY.JP.

YK: Tell us what you will focus on in the future.

YT: Until now, we have focused on developing BASE, a service for creating online shops so that anyone can easily sell products, and the company has grown into one whose services are used by about 400,000 merchants (as of May 2017). We would like to increase the value of the shopping-mall app, which makes it possible to purchase products offered by stores created with BASE. We do not want to limit our work to creating online shops.

As for PAY.JP and PAY ID, they provide an environment in which people can undertake optimal economic activities by increasing not only use of our services, the number of participating EC sites, web services, and apps but also situations when PAY ID payment can be used.

Our 10-year goal is to operate as broadly as we can on a global basis. In particular, we will seek to improve all aspects of our services that users find bothersome. In the area of payments, we will seek to improve credit analysis mechanisms using information available over the Internet, thereby providing finance opportunities for individuals who lack all access to credit of any kind (for example, they may not possess a credit card). We also intend to provide business support through social lending for merchants.

It is said that before there was money, business was conducted by exchanging goods via a barter system. After that, there was probably a period when rocks and shells were used as currency. Currency regimes almost certainly adapt to changes in the economic environment.

Even considering this history, as IT spreads and online services become deeply intertwined with people's lives, currencies may disappear in the future and society may become cashless. Japan is a safe country, and a culture of carrying cash has taken root, but as the world continues to globalize and the concept of borders weakens, it will be necessary for that culture and habit of carrying cash to change, and this will probably catalyze the continued development of online currencies.

Payments

Exchange Corporation K.K.
Representative: Russell Cummer, Founder, Director, and CEO
Company profile
Founded: March 2008
Customers: STORES.jp, Shoplist, Peach John, Fril, Yumetenbo
Exchange Corporation provides the online payment service Paidy, which does not require a credit card.

This original service is unique in that users do not need to sign up in advance, it is optimized for smartphone use (fully paperless), and there is a lump sum bill once a month.

Yoshitaka Kitao: Tell us about the history of the company.
Russell Cummer: Exchange Corporation K.K. is a FinTech company that provides the Paidy online payment service, which users do not need to sign up for in advance. After graduating from US-based Stanford University with a master's degree in financial mathematics, I worked as a bond trader at the Tokyo office of Goldman Sachs, and then founded the company. I am a Canadian, was born in Singapore, and lived half of my life in Asia, including Japan and Hong Kong. I see myself as an entrepreneur with roots in Japan.

Paidy is targeted to the EC market. As people have become accustomed to online shopping, Japan's EC market has grown to 13.8 trillion yen annually, the third largest following China and the United States. While credit cards are generally used to make payments, Japan is unique in that a large percentage of Japanese consumers prefer to use cash as opposed to credit cards (many don't even have the latter). In addition, relative to citizens of other countries in the developed world, Japanese people are hesitant to provide credit card information over the Internet. As a result, various payment methods that do not involve credit cards (cash-on-delivery [COD], payments made at convenience stores, and bank transfers) account for 40% of all EC.

YK: Tell us about your business.
RC: For COD purchases, the person generally needs to be home when the product is delivered. In addition, for payments at convenience stores and bank transfers, it is necessary to complete payment procedures at that time. Even though people themselves choose to use such methods, it cannot be denied that there are inconvenient

aspects to them. Paidy eliminates all the troubles related to paying with cash.

By simply entering their phone number and email address using their smartphone, people can begin to use the payment service just like a credit card with a "single lump-sum payment for all purchases made during a month," to be billed the following month. The required time for screening is normally several seconds. There are also other features not available when using cash, such as being able to select installment payments. It is possible to check bills and use history on the smartphone whenever one wants, and because of our outstanding user interface (UI), it is possible to conduct detailed searches of bills by simply saying something like "used 25,000 yen on a sports website."

Unique Features That Eliminate the Need for Credit Cards

RC: In addition to Paidy, there are numerous other services that extol the virtues on online payment services, but the majority of them require linking to a credit card. As such, they are not effective payment methods for people who are hesitant to record their credit card information in the cloud or who do not have a credit card at all.

Furthermore, from its introductory development phases, Paidy has been optimized for smartphones. It employs a monthly, lump-sum payment cycle, and is completely paperless, making it a mechanism that meets the greater demands of EC users who pay with cash.

Paidy's motto is "what you want, then and there," and in its current form, we provide the service based on the use of EC on smartphones, making more transactions possible, but if an innovative component technology that replaces smartphones arises in the future, we are prepared to adapt to these as well.

A Business Model That Avoids the Risk of Uncollectable Accounts

RC: Having described Paidy from the perspective of consumers, we now turn our attention to sellers.

The service is also extremely appealing for member stores that operate EC websites. For payments made with cash, the sale is not finalized until the money is actually received. This is a major difference from credit cards, whose payment is guaranteed when the customer checks out.

In general, our approach avoids certain costs associated with credit card payment systems, such as those involving the reshipment of products to people who make COD purchases but are away when the product is delivered, return procedures when fees are not paid after the product is received, and refund processes when orders are canceled.

YK: Tell us about your actual growth
RC: Paidy member merchants can execute the complete product sales flow when payment is made with cash, just like they do when a credit card is used: Checking out is the same as finalizing the transaction, and shipping is the equivalent of a complete process. In other words, the ease of use that consumers feel with Paidy means that merchants are freed from the risk of collecting payment and logistic expenses that cash payments entail. This was not a solution, however, to operational costs related to cash payments, which can be considered necessary expenses when engaging in EC in Japan.

Ours is a fundamental solution that companies that operate websites did not even hope for, but that is the appeal of Paidy. Our method generates synergies for consumers, who were waiting for a simpler, more convenient method for paying by cash, and participating merchants, who want to reduce business costs related to cash payments as much as possible. The number of users of Paidy, which was launched in October 2014, grew to 500,000 by December 31, 2016, and reached 2 million people by the end of 2017.

The Importance of a New Payment Method

RC: As the number of Paidy users increases, their distinguishing features are gradually becoming clear. One such feature is that there is steady growth in their average monthly use. An examination of changes in the amount of the first six purchases made by a population of randomly selected users revealed that the amount gradually increased each time the service was used, and by the sixth time, the amount had risen more than twofold. This is probably because of the user environment and options unavailable with cash, such as lump billing and next month payment–promoted purchases.

A second feature is the strong tendency for users to return to the platform. According to data reported by participating merchants, Paidy has the greatest repeat user rate among users of the various payment methods, and it boasts an overall average repeat rate of 20%.

The third distinguishing point is more of an important discovery for participating merchants than a trait of users: Paidy helps participating merchants capture new customers. According to feedback from participating merchants, about 40% of Paidy users are first-time buyers, which is greater than that for other payment methods.

In general, our experience thus far indicates that consumers who start to use Paidy quickly become accustomed to credit card–like platform features such as the unique UI, and are inclined to make active use of the service, which consolidates all of their buying behavior. Participating merchants can win highly loyal customers without being burdened by credit risk. As such, the service creates a win-win relationship for customers and participating merchants.

Issuers and Acquirers

RC: Paidy's business model is based on both B2B and B2B2C service, where we collect a payment service fee from companies that operate EC sites that target consumers. We are gradually expanding into the C2C field through various efforts such as signing up sites that facilitate product sales between consumers.

Therefore, the priority in the business strategy for now is encouraging more EC sites to become participating merchants. Because our experience to date suggests that once Paidy is adopted, it accounts for at least about 10% of total purposes (share of payment), Paidy expects to increase revenue through the payment of fees on 5 billion yen in sales for an EC site with annual sales of 50 billion yen, 10 billion yen in sales for EC sites with annual sales of 100 billion yen, and so on. This will make it possible to increase our user base. In other words, activities to capture new participating merchants directly leads to new clients. Just as is the case in the credit card industry, our business can be viewed as one that serves as both the issuer and acquirer.

Quick Screening Using an AI Engine

RC: For the payment industry, managing bad debts is as important an issue as capturing new participating merchants. When a transaction is completed on a site that uses Paidy, we become legally obligated to pay the purchasers' debt to the seller.

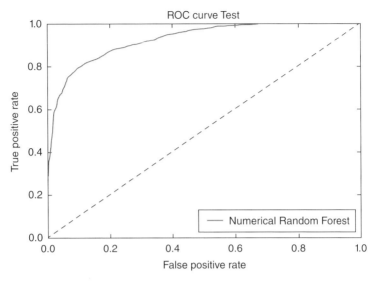

FIGURE 4.7 Machine Learning to Prevent Authorized Use
Source: Exchange Corporation.

We bill the purchaser (Paidy user) later, but if the purchaser does not have the ability to pay, that amount becomes a bad debt for us, and it is ultimately recorded as a loss.

In order to limit losses associated with such a policy, we conduct extensive credit screening. After users enter their phone number and email address, the process takes only a few seconds to complete and the consumer can then immediately begin using the service. An AI engine and algorithm makes the quick screening possible (Figure 4.7).

Here, we seek to limit both the incidence of unauthorized use, along with the speed of on-boarding users onto the platform. It is not an exaggeration to say that the evaluation algorithm, which not only checks against several databases but also employs our proprietary machine learning, is one of our most valuable strategic assets.

Because of weak economic growth and low interest rates throughout the world, bonds are no longer unilaterally viewed as safe assets, and diversified investing across the four traditional assets classes (domestic stocks, domestic bonds, overseas stocks, and overseas bonds) is no longer a practice accepted on pure faith. It is my opinion that under these conditions, collaboration with financial institutions centered on the provision of financial services to Paidy's customer base has unlimited potential.

YK: What is the future outlook?

RC: I would like to touch on our objectives for 10 years into the future. As shown in Figure 4.8, a breakdown of EC purchases patterns reveals that half of the people in their twenties and thirties use their smartphones; a reality that matches the fact this age group is our core demographic.

Under these circumstances, we believe it to be almost certain that smartphones will overtake computers and become the dominant tool for EC purchases in 10 years. If so, our business should expand accordingly.

We envision that the financial needs of existing Paidy users will become more diverse as they transition from their twenties into their thirties, and from their thirties into their forties, because they will form families and their work will qualitatively change. Paidy will change to meet those needs.

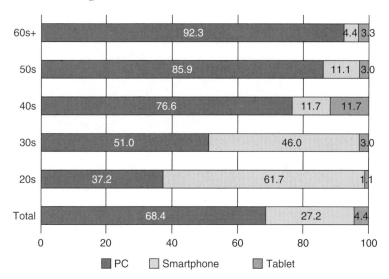

FIGURE 4.8 EC Use by Age Group and Access Method
Source: Material created by Exchange Corporation using "Trends in Online Payments and Smartphone Payments" released by the Consumer Affairs Agency.

Our long-term vision for Paidy is to develop it into a concierge service for all money matters, first by making a virtual credit card (cardless card), then an online wallet, and so on. We are also examining expanding abroad. Even before discussing the percentage of people who have credit cards, there are still countries in Asia where a small percentage of people have bank accounts, and there is a very strong potential demand for the services that we provide.

Payments

Origami Inc.
  Representative: Yoshiki Yasui, Director and President
  Company profile
    Founded: 2012
    Number of customers: 1,500 companies
    Example customers: Marui, AOKI, Hankyu Department Store, LoFt,
      Nihon Kotsu
    Origami Inc. develops and operates smartphone payment and EC systems. With the mission of bringing consumers closer to shops through the smartphone, Origami offers consumers efficient payment methods and supplies merchants with support for effective sales promotions.

Yoshitaka Kitao: Tell us about the history of the company.
Yoshiki Yasui: I was born in Toronto, returned to Japan when I was 10 years old, and started to invest when I was 19, which provided me with business experiences at a very young age.
         After that, I worked as an M&A advisor at Lehman Brothers and was involved in investing in startup companies at three different offices (United States, Japan, and China) of Silicon Valley–based Doll Capital Management (DCM Ventures). I firmly believed at that time that, as the Internet expanded, the financial industry would develop a new business model. I founded Origami Inc. With these opportunities in mind.
         Figure 4.9 outlines the history of the company since its founding.

February 2012	Established Origami
March 2013	Raised a total of 500 million yen through a third-party allotment to KDDI and DAC
April 2013	Launched EC service
April 2015	Raised a total of 1.6 billion yen through a third-party allotment to SoftBank, Credit Saison, and Mr. Makoto Takano
May 2016	Officially launched store payment service Origami Pay
November 2016	Established a business tie-up with Alipay, China's largest electronic payment service

FIGURE 4.9 Origami's History
Source: Origami Inc.

Giving Smartphones a Wallet Feel

YK: Tell us about your business.

YY: With a corporate mission of "empowering consumers and businesses to come closer together through 'commerce'," we provide a fund transfer platform.

In particular, we have introduced the smartphone payment service Origami Pay for brick-and-mortar stores, and an EC service via a smartphone app (iOS and Android).

Origami Pay is a service that consumers can use as a convenient payment method via their smartphones like a wallet. New merchants can use it as a mechanism to conduct sales promotions that directly foster customer loyalty, while simultaneously informing customers with appropriate product explanations and special campaign notifications.

When introducing the service, consumers download the Origami app, which makes it possible to make payments by simply registering a credit card (Visa, MasterCard, and other card brands are expected to be steadily added).

Participating merchants can introduce the service by installing our proprietary merchant application Origami for Business, through simple settings. POS registers already installed in stores can be used as it is, because there is no need to change them.

A Service That Does Not Entail Fixed Expenses

YY: Merchants on the Origami platform are relieved of fixed costs such as initial expenses and monthly fees. Merchants do pay a fee for the smartphone payment service (3.25% of the purchase amount) and an online sales fee for EC services (10% of purchase amount).

In the future, we plan to provide sales promotion functions, such as a premium service for a monthly fee and optional use fee.

For consumers, payment and EC service fees do not apply.

YK: Tell us about your actual growth.

YY: The app has been highly praised for its innovative design and user appeal. This is evidenced by various facts, including that in 2013, when the service was introduced, it was selected as the year's best app on Apple's App Store, as well as the most attention-drawing app on Google Play.

Our services are used by numerous stores, including such leading Japanese commercial facilities as Mitsukoshi Isetan, Hankyu Department Store, Marui Group, restaurants chains including Kentucky Fried Chicken, major lifestyle general goods stores such as LoFt and Francfranc, Nihon Kotsu taxis, clothing stores, movie theaters, and beauty product companies. The number of merchants that have introduced either the payment service or EC service has surpassed 4,800.

Furthermore, in November 2016, we launched a business tie-up with Alipay, the largest electronic payment service in China.

This collaboration will make it possible for Chinese visitors to Japan to use Alipay at stores that have introduced Origami Pay, and by doing so, we expand our client's revenue base. Chinese visitors often undertake multiple trips to Japan and can become repeat customers. Stores that are new to Origami can access the Alipay system through Origami Pay.

YK: Can you give us a success example?

YY: Companies that have introduced our services have praised it for "increasing customer convenience and raising customer satisfaction," and we have built strong partnerships with these entities that involve continued and expanded use of the system.

One merchant that introduced Origami Pay is the suit store and clothing retailer AOKI, which introduced the service at its Ikebukuro Higashiguchi and Shinjuku Higashiguchi stores. It immediately and smoothly operated at the register, and this increased the shopping convenience for customers. As of, October 11, 2016, the company began to introduce the system into its 71 stores in Tokyo, Kanagawa and Saitama[4]. By year-end, the company expanded the introduction to its 564 stores throughout Japan.[5]

Developing the Field of Retail Online Market Payment Field

YK: Tell us about the business environment.

YY: It is said that Japan's 13.8-trillion-yen EC market is in a growth phase. Placing this figure in perspective, the offline, (brick-and-mortar) retail market is about 130 trillion yen.

According to the "2017 Telecommunications Whitepaper" released by the Ministry of Internal Affairs and Communications, 1.3 billion smartphones were shipped globally by 2014, and shipments are projected to grow at the robust average pace of 10.7% annually. In Japan, 71% of Japanese own a smartphone and

---

[4] This includes the Inadazutsumi store (Kanagawa) and Wako Hikarigaoka store (Saitama), but not the Mina Machida store.

[5] Stores that have introduced Origami Pay as of December 1, 2016. All AOKI stores in Japan except for the following: Mina Machida store, Mina Tsudanuma store, Ito-Yokado Yanaizu store, Ito-Yokado Tsukuno store, AEON Town Tomiominami store, AEON Town Tasaki store, Terasso Himeji store, Sasebo Gobangai store, Mita Tenjin store.

ownership of tablets has quickly grown to 39%.[6] Therefore, the diffusion rate of smartphones among consumers is already high.

The payment technology of the retail offline market, however, continues to lag behind (Figure 4.10). It is our belief that the introduction of the smartphone has created a foundation for change.

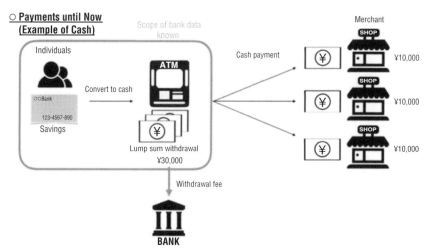

[1] Information interruption
Information on the saving balance is interrupted when money is withdrawn as cash and it is impossible to ascertain the final payment site.

[2] Declining fee income
For various reasons, including ATMs that do not charge fees for withdrawals, fees will probably drop to zero in the future.

FIGURE 4.10 Payments Until Now (Example of Cash)
Source: Origami Inc.

Furthermore, as the number of entrants into the smartphone payment market increases, the overall market will grow, which will accelerate the rate that users become aware of and understand smartphone-based payments. We believe that as such Origami possesses a golden opportunity to promote its diffusion among consumers and merchants.

Preventing unauthorized use in the payment field

YY: Government entities including the Financial Services Agency have issued warnings related to the use of credit cards at brick-and-mortar stores, including leaks of information obtained from credit

---

[6] 2016 Fixed-point Media Survey released by Hakuhodo DY Media Partners' Institute of Media Environment, http://mekanken.com/cms/wp-content/uploads/2017/07/846a7e37a4c75 9999b6d3ee9fe2fea2e.pdf

card readers and improper use of stored and managed credit card data. The industry must deal with these issues. It is possible that the same problems could arise for payments made with smartphones, and some people have commented on their hopes that Internet technology can be used as one countermeasure.

In light of these conditions, Origami will create a new business-technology model for the off-line retail market, based upon expanding the use of the Internet in the payment field.

YK: Tell us what you will focus on in the future.

YY: We believe that with our technology, Origami Pay, beyond its role in the payment and EC industry, can be applied across the overall finance field of finance, offering functions relating to such pro-cesses as sending, saving, accumulating, borrowing, and lending.

For example, banks (top entities in the savings field), face the perennial issue of is maintaining existing business lines, while con-temporaneously developing a new business-technology model. It can also be argued that this is one of the reasons that there is growing expectations for FinTech.

We will form partnerships with banks and seamlessly link existing bank accounts to Origami Pay payments using our Inter-net technology and knowledge, which will make it possible to smoothly expand from payments to savings (Figure 4.11).

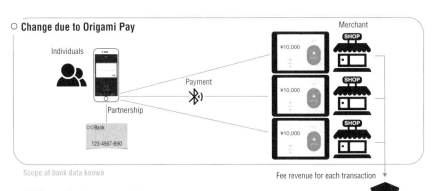

○ **Change due to Origami Pay**

Individuals

Payment

Partnership

Merchant

SHOP

Scope of bank data known

Fee revenue for each transaction

BANK

[1] Accumulating payment data

Clearly ascertain the final payment site—what user paid for what where

→Data-based marketing (sales promotion of financial products for individuals and year-end gifts and lending for corporations)

[2] New efforts using participating merchant fee as source of funds

As for the fee for participating merchants, payment via bank account entails a relatively low fee compared to that for credit cards. The difference is an incentive to use bank accounts.

FIGURE 4.11 Change Due to Origami Pay

Source: Origami Inc.

Following is the actual example of partnership dynamics with banks. Under the current framework, Origami payments are charged exclusively against the credit card that the consumer registers. This will be revised, and it will also be possible for users to make payments from bank accounts.

Banks Can Acquire Customer Payment Data

YY: Banks linking Origami Pay to customer accounts also gain the benefits associated with the accumulation of newly available forms of client payment data, allowing them to better understand what customers buy, where they buy it, and at what price, and for what purpose.

This will probably lead to new data use models, taking the form of financial instrument promotion programs, year-end gifts for individual customers and different forms of corporate lending.

The same logic applies across multiple financial business segments. We will focus our energy on business models that generate synergies between consumers and businesses, and that provide financial services that bring consumers closer through commerce.

Payments

Liquid
Representative: Yasuhiro Kuda, Director
Company profile
Founded: 2013
Partners: Several dozen companies, including major corporations (joint partner research).
Example customers: Huis Ten Bosch, Aeon Bank, KDDI, Prince Hotel
With the business vision of "creating a natural world in which people prove their own identity," Liquid has developed faster, more efficient biometric authentication technologies, utilizing image and big data analysis.

Yoshitaka Kitao: Tell us about the history of the company.
Yasuhiro Kuda: I studied financial engineering and started my career in investment banking. This career path allowed me to gain experience working with numerous companies. The next step in my career path involved working with venture companies.

It was at this point that I began to think about future changes in society and felt the importance of IoT – in particular the concept of users unconsciously accessing services in a more natural environment in which sensors actively acquire information. Furthermore, when YouTube and Instagram began to grow in popularity, I began to think that there would be a need for technology to conduct searches, not by having people input text, but by using sensing, which involves measuring things with sensors and searching for information from within images. The era when devices such as computers, tablets, and smartphones are necessary is over, and it is now an era of services that make use of sensing. This was the concept that became the genesis for creating the company. In pursuit of this idea, various companies and research institutions moved forward with the development of machine learning and deep learning, which created an artificial intelligence (AI) boom. In response to this development, it began to look like the future would be an era of image analysis.

Biometric Authentication That Links the Real World to the Internet

Kuda: While providing support for startup companies, I came to feel deeply that an authentication method using a scheme other than the traditional ID and password would be indispensable for linking the "real world" to the Internet. I felt that the field of biometric authentication that makes impersonation impossible would grow over the next 10 to 20 years.

Our research in the field of biometric authentication led to the following discovery. In Japan, fingerprints are used to make criminal investigations, and I noticed that weight is placed on a one-to-one comparison.

When using biometric authentication for payments and identification, a technology that makes it possible to instantaneously search vast amounts of data, as opposed to conducting one-to-one comparisons, is required. Here, we applied image analysis technology used for automated driving to the mapping of images, and transformed this data into efficiently stored, irreversible data units. At the same time, methods to efficiently store data were examined via machine learning, and we succeeded in developing an algorithm to quickly search fingerprints using a system based on one-to-mass comparison, not one-to-one comparison.

Response to Biometric Authentication Using Fingerprints, Iris, Veins, and the Face

Kuda: The current state of Liquid Inc. came into being in iterations. There are various biometric authentication methods, such as using fingerprints, irises, and veins, and many companies specialize in one of these methods, but we have developed algorithms able to handle four types of biometric authentication (fingerprints, irises, veins, and face).

We have divided our operation into three functional corporate units—Liquid Japan, established to conduct sales and marketing in Japan; Recreation Lab, organized as a research institute for basic technology; and MyCity a specialized unit designed to facilitate the use of image analysis and other technologies in managing a metropolis.

The original Liquid team was engineers who, in their twenties, worked at companies that demanded "explosive power," such as game companies. For online game development, it is necessary to provide continual development services 24 hours a day in order to add functions and make fixes. We believed that if we continued work on the development of products such as biometric authentication, we might have lost our position.

However, there are high entry barriers to the market for component technology, which not everyone can do, and, as we grew older, I considered that development of component technology as the only path for us.

Kitao: Tell us about your business.
Kuda: Our business is extremely diverse. For example, an entity making use of biometric authentication systems is a Sri Lankan resort hotel, Huis Ten Bosch, Yuigahama Beach House (Kamakura-shi, Kanagawa). Furthermore, there are plans to broadly introduce store registers that can handle reduced tax rates, and include a biometric authentication payment system, which will make it possible to make payments with biometric authentication in several tens of thousands of locations throughout Japan in 2017.

Other actual cases of authentication systems in place include the introduction of a fingerprint system to replace student IDs at the Mapua Institute of Technology in the Philippines. In addition, we are undertaking other activities, including not only conducting a verification test for online banks to make it possible to withdraw money from ATMs using only biometric authentication, but also creating a platform for *hands-free tourism*. This was selected as the Ministry of Economy, Trade and Industry's omotenashi (hospitality) platform – a system that makes checking in at hotels and traditional Japanese-style lodgings, and paying at surrounding facilities seamless for foreigners visiting Japan.

We also plan to introduce various other services using information obtained from image and video analysis, including one to propose clothing appropriate for the shape of the user's face and one that recommends driving routes.

These solutions were selected for two awards: the ICT Innovation Creation Challenge Program (i-Challenge!), presented by the Ministry of Internal Affairs and Communications; and the top Lab Selection award Advanced IoT Project Selection Committee within the IoT Promotion Consortium, presented by the Ministry of Economy, Trade and Industry and the Ministry of Internal Affairs and Communications. In this way, the government is facilitating the expansion of our business.

The main source of revenue for Liquid is payment for system fees. With a biometric authentication system, users can make payments by simply passing their finger over a reader, and they can select the payment method they prefer, either prepaid or postpaid (bank account withdrawal or credit card) types are available.

Furthermore, we are examining the introduction of payment methods that employ bank APIs. Merchants can use Liquid for a fee that is less than that they pay for their existing payment system.

It was possible to do so because the system significantly reduces the cost of unauthorized use due to impersonation and forgery. These costs are a significant drain on the economy; between January and September 2016, the total cost of unauthorized use of credit cards surpassed 10 billion yen.[7]

Biometric authentication renders impersonation difficult, so its application dramatically reduces the amount of unauthorized use. In turn, these savings can be passed along in the form of reduced pricing for the service.

Kitao: Tell us about actual cases when the system was introduced, and the business environment.

Kuda:

Example 1: Hotel check-in using biometric authentication (Ikebukuro Sunshine City Prince Hotel).

The Inns and Hotels Act stipulates that when visitors to Japan check in at hotels and traditional Japanese lodgings, they must

---

[7] Figures on unauthorized use of credit cards was obtained from the Consumer Credit Association, http://www.j-credit.or.jp/download/news20160331.pdf.

present their passport, and the lodging must make a copy of the passport and store it. Therefore, it takes about five minutes for each guest to check in. Until now, foreign tourists on bus tours flooded lobbies, resulting in long lines and wait times at the front during the check-in process.

With the cooperation of government authorities and in-house attorneys, we have eliminated the need for guests to present their passport, and for the hotel to store copies. The specific technology involved is called the system to eliminate Regulatory Gray Zones, which used Liquid's biometric authentication system to check the passport information of guests. Furthermore, it is the judgment of the Ministry of Health, Labor and Welfare that this practice is compliant with the terms of the Inns and Hotels Act.

This made it possible to reduce the time it takes to check in by 80%–90% at the Ikebukuro Sunshine City Prince Hotel. Although the verification test only transpired for a limited time, a little fewer than 1,000 foreign visitors used the system, but they commented that "check-in was simple and convenient."

After that, there were several developments, including revisions to the Inns and Hotels Act, and we were able to eliminate numerous inconveniences using our technology, which led us to pioneer this important field.

Example 2: Hands-free payments at the beach (beach stores at Yuigahama)

One problem people face when at the beach is how to pay when they visit beach stores. Many people who visit the beach do not keep their wallets on their person, and they must retrieve them when they want to buy food, drink or other items from beach stores. Some consumers probably avoid beach purchases because retrieving their wallets is bothersome.

With our payment system, users who first register their phone number and fingerprint can enjoy themselves, eat and drink without having anything in hand. At the store, average per-guest spending was 1,500 yen before the payment system was introduced, but increased to more than 3,000 yen after the system was introduced. During the July to August time frame we examined, and about 2,000 people visited the store.

For these cases, even though availability was limited in time and space, thousands of people used the service. This indicates that the demand for the application of biometric authentication is diverse and substantial.

In recent years, biometric authentication has become common, as smartphones come equipped with fingerprint authentication functions, and computers come with facial recognition functions, and it is expected that this trend will accelerate in the future.

Kitao: Tell us what you will focus on in the future.

Kuda: The world we are striving to create is one in which (1) only individuals themselves can prove who they are and (2) there is safety and convenience in conducting commerce. The combination of these features with the IoT creates what is referred to as the *Internet of Persons (IoP)*.

This is a word we coined that refers to a society in which people are identified using various types of physical information, not "things," and "people" are analyzed and identified using sensor-based technology, without relying on tablets and terminals.

There are currently various situations when people need to present their driver's license or insurance card in order to confirm their identity when completing procedures or applications. Biometric authentication technology is probably one way to identify people and it achieves this objective at places such as government offices and banks without using driver's licenses or insurance cards. This functionality can be of vital importance to individuals trying to access lifelines when a major disaster occurs.

Many consumers carry various cards (credit cards, ATM cards, point cards, etc.) in order to increase the convenience of daily life, but the more cards people have, the greater the risk they will be lost. If they could all be tied to biometric information, and managed and accessed via fingerprint authentication when necessary, it would probably dramatically increase convenience and guarantee safety. If this can be achieved, it will be possible to make things truly hands-free. Before long, our technology may allow consumers to operate without cash or key.

There is arguably greater need for services such as ours in regions including Southeast Asia and Africa, where the use of credit cards and similar methods for paying is not widespread and many people do not have bank accounts.

As such, we are launching a business through various partnerships in developing countries through which we hope to promote our business by meeting local needs in the future.

In order to realize an IoP society, we want to increase the number of locations where the service can be used, and move the business forward to create a new society both within and outside of Japan.

Cryptocurrency

QUOINE
Representative: Kariya Mike Kayamori, Director
Company profile
  Founded: 2014
  Partners: Traders Holdings
  Partnership examples: Internet initiative (joint verification test)
  QUOINE operates cryptocurrency exchanges in Japan and countries throughout Asia. A distinguishing feature of QUOINE is its B2B business model for providing exchange systems as white label and OEM services. Three companies have already introduced the service.

Yoshitaka Kitao: Tell us about the history of the company.

Kariya Mike Kayamori: Blockchain and cryptocurrencies are one of the truly revolutionary technology breakthroughs developed since the advent of the Internet. Until now, for countries, governments, and the financial industry, including central banks, were responsible for guaranteeing credit and trust, the foundation of all services. Blockchains and cryptocurrencies make it possible to authenticate and guarantee transactions outside of the realm of government and politically organized structures.

Internationality, Diversity, Resilience

KMK: I would like to quickly introduce myself before discussing the company's business. There were two major factors that have had a major impact on who I am today.

The first is internationality and diversity. I had never lived in Japan until I started university. Although born in Japan, I lived in Colombia for three years, Canada five years, and New Jersey and Los Angeles for nine years. This experience enabled me to develop the ability to accept and embrace diversity. In addition, I learned the importance of communication and resilience. My father died of cancer when I was in the fifth grade in Los Angeles and my life in the United States without want suddenly disappeared. I found myself in a one-parent household in a foreign country. We did not have the choice of returning to Japan, and my mother worked two jobs to keep her three sons in school through college. During that time, I developed a strong spirit to never give in to poverty or any adversity.

After that, I studied at Tokyo University and Harvard Business School, worked at Mitsubishi Corporation, a US-based venture capital company, and then SoftBank, and finally established

QUOINE Pte. Ltd. The origin of QUOINE is an intersection of chance and inevitability.

At that time, I was living in Singapore and managing the Asian branch of SoftBank's Overseas Business Strategy Office. There, I came upon a joint venture between Singapore Telecommunications and India-based Bharti Group, and I happened to get to know Mario Gomez-Lozada, the co-founder of QUOINE, through a friend. He was resigning as the chief information officer of Credit Suisse Japan and considering launching a company.

I had previously been interested in cryptocurrencies and blockchains. Mario and I saw eye to eye on these topics and I convinced him to establish the company.

At that time, I was still working at SoftBank, but my role was limited. I was at most an angel advisor for the establishment of the company, but I was unable to restrain my passion. I resigned from SoftBank at the end of March 2016 and took up the position of CEO of QUOINE.

Foundation of Financial Services Is Liquidity

KMK: QUOINE provides a financial service whose core is blockchain technology; the initial service has been a cryptocurrency exchange. We provide an exchange that makes it possible to trade cryptocurrencies, such as Bitcoin and Ethereum.

At the time, there were fewer than 10 companies in Japan that provided exchange and trading services for cryptocurrencies, but QUOINE's business model was a B2B one. In other words, those cryptocurrency exchange operators, companies, and financial business operators involved in the cryptocurrency trading business are all potential QUOINE customers. We are aiming to be a so-called exchange of exchanges.

Cryptocurrencies are all digital, as the name implies, and their core technology is blockchain. When operating an exchange, processing capability to execute trades, performance, availability, redundancy, and security are all important, but it is also important to be knowledgeable about blockchain and wallet technology, which is always evolving.

It is unrealistic for existing financial business operators that provide cryptocurrency selling services to its customers to independently develop everything in advance. That is what QUOINE provides. As a white-label producer or OEM (one that provides service under the brand name of the customer), we offer exchange services such as a turnkey solution (system that can be immediately used), and our partner companies can provide cryptocurrency services to their customers within a couple of months.

Furthermore, we consider liquidity–that is, ease of exchange–to be the foundation of financial services. It is necessary to provide perpetual liquidity such that when customers want to purchase or sell a cryptocurrency, they can do so immediately. During the Lehman Brothers collapse or amid the financial panic in Japan in the second half of the 1990s, market participants faced the problem of declining liquidity owing to a number of factors, including the credit crunch. QUOINE is focused on this. In the non-virtual foreign exchange markets, consortiums of global banks provide liquidity as counterparties, but with cryptocurrencies, there is no such counterparty. QUOINE provides the liquidity, in collaboration with various parties, including independent market makers and overseas exchanges.

However, QUOINE is not a system vendor. We do not charge for system development costs, and so on, but earn income through revenue sharing and from fees for each transaction. In other words, our model is based on growing with partners as their businesses grow and the fee revenues increase rather than earning compensation for traditional development and labor.

YK: What are the distinguishing features of the business environment?
KMK: Japan, as it happens, is a potential cryptocurrency superpower. It will probably become the number one cryptocurrency country within several years.

For example, foreign exchange is an asset similar to cryptocurrencies. The volume of retail Foreign (FX) trading in Japan totaled 5 quadrillion yen in 2015, the largest in the world. Japanese individual investors are referred to as Mrs. Watanabe, because they trade so much that they impact global foreign exchange markets.[8] It is certainly feasible for currencies to account for 10% of all transactions.

Furthermore, Japan is a point system (variable awards for engaging in transactions activities) superpower. One widely understood example of this is frequent flyer miles. In addition to common points such as T points, Rakuten points, and ponta, there are numerous other points provided by various companies and services. Here, customers are extremely literate about points and make detailed reviews of at what rate points are awarded and when they expire. Its behavior regarding this construct is unique among the world's nations.

It is my opinion that points are simply another type of cryptocurrency. However, for those who seek to accumulate them, there

[8] https://news.bitcoin.com/worlds-largest-bitcoin-exchange-bitflyer-expands-into-us-market/.

is the risk that the rate points at which are earned and expire can be changed, whenever, or that the sponsor company could go bankrupt. Because blockchain, which is used for Bitcoin (BTC) and other cryptocurrencies, is managed in a dispersed fashion by tens of thousands of economic entities throughout the world, there risk of bankruptcy, forgery, and so on is reduced. The use of points is limited to Japan, but cryptocurrencies can be used throughout the world. If people could use an exchange in any country they visited, it could be possible to exchange the cryptocurrency to the legal currency of that country, and in the future, it may be possible to pay for things using cryptocurrencies themselves.

YK: Tell us how the business is progressing.

KMK: QUOINE's cryptocurrency business is recording dramatically more than projected rates of expansion. Rapid growth has continued since the launch of the business. Monthly trading volume was 54 when the business was officially launched in July 2014. In July 2016, two years later, monthly volume reached 1.40 million BTC, or 98 billion yen at an exchange rate of 70 thousand yen per BTC. This is a 26,000-fold growth.

Current monthly trading volume is 50–100 billion yen, and a number that is expected to grow into the trillions. Furthermore, the business is growing not only in Japan but also throughout the world. Bitcoin/yen currency pair accounts for more than 60% of QUOINE's trading volume, followed by the US dollar and the Indonesia rupiah. There is also strong growth for the Philippine peso and the Singapore dollar.

When developing a global strategy, it is important to take into consideration various factors, such as each country's laws and regulations, opening bank accounts and human network, and it is difficult for a single company to do it all. We are moving forward with our global strategy in collaboration with various partners. We will be able to quickly expand platform use if the B2B business takes off.

Furthermore, we have yet to do any advertising or marketing for QUOINE. The mobile app has yet to be optimized, and the B2B business was just launched. In order to ensure resources are sufficient to keep up with the growth of the company, we raised a total of 2 billion yen and to have built systems inside and outside of the company.

YK: Tell us about your customers and business partners.

KMK: As discussed above, QUOINE is focused on B2B operations. The information has not been made public, but two companies in

Japan are already using our services to provide cryptocurrency trading services. We are providing one company with a full-package OEM product and the other company with liquidity. We have also entered the final stage of discussions regarding partnership with several Japanese financial institutions. Across these collaborations, we are exercising great caution in selecting our partners.

Financial services must, of course, be safe because the money and assets of customers are involved, but they must also assume a public and social nature.

We are not pursuing growth at all costs as some Internet startup companies have done in the past, particularly at the expense of conducting business in a disciplined manner. The services and functions we provide lead to customer satisfaction, and when that satisfaction grows into trust, the B2B business will be a success.

YK: Tell us about partnerships and collaborations with financial institutions.

KMK: Interest in cryptocurrencies is growing to such an extent that it is covered in newspapers and other media every day. Many people want to purchase cryptocurrencies using their accounts at the financial institutions, online FX trading service providers, and online securities companies with which they have grown accustomed; they are reluctant to embrace new trading platforms, a process that involves various steps, including opening an account at a new cryptocurrency business operator. Even though my father-in-law is interested in purchasing bitcoins, he does not appear to have the desire to register with a cryptocurrency business operator – even if the entity in question is his son-in-law's company.

I want QUOINE to help create an ecosystem in which anyone in the world can easily trade cryptocurrencies. We do not plan on undertaking any vertical mergers or competing with existing financial institutions with large customer bases.

As of April 2017, existing financial institutions can enter the cryptocurrency business if they register with the Financial Services Agency. Offering large financial institutions opportunities to trade cryptocurrencies in a simple, safe, and reliable manner is one of our fiduciary responsibilities.

However, it is extremely risky for financial institutions to make upfront investments in markets where growth is uncertain. There is a need to understand blockchain and cold wallets (system for storing cryptocurrencies offline), and, given the rise of Bitcoin and new cryptocurrencies such as Ethereum, it is not easy for financial institutions to independently develop and bring in house the development of systems that can handle all these rapidly expanding markets.

For these financial institutions, QUOINE provides not only a full package as white label (OEM) but also liquidity. Existing financial institutions can tell their customers that "they can trade Japanese and overseas stocks, investment trusts, bonds, foreign exchange, futures, and even cryptocurrencies.

YK: Tell us what you will focus on in the future.

KMK: Various issues, including ones related to laws, regulations, and taxes, have been resolved and Japan is leading the world in developing of a cryptocurrency infrastructure.

Laws related to cryptocurrencies were approved in May 2016, and they came into effect in April 2017. Cryptocurrency business operators are able to officially provide services by registering with the Financial Services Agency.

Ensuring comprehensive compliance – including issues such as confirming the identity of individuals and preventing money laundering is vital, of course, and this is one of QUOINE's strengths. Most of the members of the QUOINE management team come from financial institutions, and the chief compliance officer (CCO) has more than 20 years of experience at one of the leading banks in the world.

Furthermore, the question of whether the consumption tax is applicable to cryptocurrencies, one point of concern, was resolved. Trading of cryptocurrencies is not subject to the consumption tax. Japan's decision in this regard is consistent with tax policy across the globe.

QUOINE provides financial services based on blockchain and features a B2B ecosystem for cryptocurrency exchanges. Given these value propositions, as well as a stable liquidity profile, we are entering a new growth phase.

Particularly in Asia, there are numerous countries where a majority of the population does not have bank accounts, and it is difficult for existing financial institutions to enter these markets. In these countries, the cost of operating offices such as headquarters and branch offices, and running legacy systems developed around mainframes are impediments, and they cannot quickly provide financial services that are inexpensive and appropriate for the time.

In 10 years, we would like to provide financial services across the globe and to contribute to worldwide economic development, while working with existing financial institutions and FinTech startup companies, using blockchains and clouds.

Blockchain

SBI Ripple Asia
  Representative: Takashi Okita, Director
  Company profile
    Founded: 2016
    Customers: 61 banks (banks that are members of the consortium)
    Partnership examples: Mitsubishi UFJ Financial Group, Mizuho
      Financial Group, Resona Bank
  SBI Ripple Asia is introducing the next-generation settlement platform that leverages blockchain technology throughout Asia. The company was established as a joint venture of SBI Holdings and US-based Ripple. In October 2016, these entities launched The Japan Bank Consortium.

Yoshitaka Kitao: Tell us about the history of the company.
Takashi Okita: As the name suggests, the company is a joint venture of SBI Holdings and US-based Ripple, and is responsible for expanding business in Japan and Asia.

Founded in 2012, US-based Ripple is a global leader in blockchain technologies. Although established only a short time ago, the combined company employs over 200 people, mainly in San Francisco, and has expanded globally with offices in New York, London, Luxemburg, Sydney, Singapore, and Mumbai.

The vision of Ripple is to enable the world to move money like information moves today, which we define as the *Internet of Value (IoV)*.

Information today can travel around the world at low cost. Before the Internet, information was exchanged, particularly between countries, using international phone calls, telex, and satellite broadcasts. These processes were expensive and access was limited. Now, information can be exchanged by anyone at a low cost using the web, email, and so on. Even video can be sent and received throughout the world in real time. Information has acquired greater freedom because of the Internet, and the amount of data exchanged has dramatically increased.

Furthermore, even before the advent of the Internet, inefficiencies related to loading and unloading ships were eliminated at ports through the use of containers and standardization, and this dramatically reduced logistic cost. The volume of shipments throughout the world, therefore, rose dramatically and globalization accelerated.

Similar to what has already occurred, Ripple wants value to be exchanged as quickly as information is today. This is exactly the IoV that Ripple is aiming to create.

Ripple is the third company that Chris Larsen, the cofounder, has established. His other two companies, E-Loan and Prosper, were also pioneering concepts. He successfully exited them both to fully recover his investment, truly making him a serial entrepreneur in the field of FinTech. Furthermore, blockchains were a major topic at the 2016 World Economic Forum, and he has been spearheading the debate ever since.

All three companies founded by Chris Larsen, including Ripple, were established as joint ventures with the SBI Group. For some of these companies, the business model was customized to make it appropriate for the Japanese business environment, and they were successful for not only the founder of the company but also its investors and customers as well.

The sense of trust that developed between the heads of the two companies over the almost 20 years of working together is the main reason that SBI was designated as a joint venture partner when Ripple decided to focus on its expansion into Asia. Furthermore, to make use of the network in Asian markets of which SBI boasts, SBI Ripple Asia plans to not only introduce xCurrent to the markets in Asia (including Japan) but also to launch an Asian proprietary business that leverages its advanced technologies.

I serve as the representative director of SBI Ripple Asia and I am a cofounder of VeriTrans Inc., a pioneer in the field of digital payments. I have been a leader in the FinTech industry for almost two decades. I served as CEO of the company through 2015 and as the first director of the EC Payment Forum, an industry organization.

After taking the company public in 2004, I launched joint projects/joint ventures in countries such as China, India, and Indonesia, starting with China UnionPay in 2008. I promoted the expansion into Asia, took a company public in Hong Kong in 2013, and was a driving force in the payment market in Asia.

Since 2014, I have served at various entities, including as an expert committee of the Financial System Council, and have focused more on academic activities. However, I took this position as representative when the company was founded in May 2016.

YK: Tell us about your business.
TO: Ripple's business is focused on providing one frictionless experience for cross-border payments through an enterprise blockchain solution and on-demand liquidity via digital asset settlement. There are over 100 financial institutions that have joined Ripple's growing network RippleNet, many of which are in some stage of commercial deployment. Rather than a constellation of disparate

technologies, unstandardized communications and centralized networks, RippleNet is a decentralized, global network of banks that send and receive payments via Ripple's distributed financial technology – providing real-time messaging and settlement of transactions. RippleNet is based on an agreement between Ripple and network participants – all of which utilize the same technology and adhere to a consistent set of payment rules and standards.

RippleNet banks benefit from the robust connectivity, standardized technology and rich data attachments with each payment. Ripple's distributed financial technology outperforms today's infrastructure by driving down costs, increasing processing speeds and delivering end-to-end visibility into payment fees, timing and delivery.

Ripple's software, xCurrent, enables banks to differentiate themselves by offering new cross-border payments services while lowering their total cost of settlement. The solution is specifically designed to meet the needs of banks by fitting within their existing risk, compliance, and information security frameworks. Ripple's software is installed within the bank's infrastructure and is built to interface with the bank's systems using an API interface or through a translation layer that can consume traditional payment message formats to compress the integration time frame into weeks.

All members of RippleNet are connected through Ripple's standardized technology, xCurrent. xCurrent is the first, global real-time gross settlement (RTGS) system that enables banks to message and settle their transactions with increased speed, transparency, and efficiency across RippleNet's global footprint of banks and payment providers.

The solution is built around ILP, an open, neutral protocol that enables inter-operation between different ledgers and payments networks. The solution offers a cryptographically secure, end-to-end payment flow with transaction immutability and information redundancy. It is designed to comply with each bank's risk, privacy and compliance requirements. The software is architected to fit within banks' existing infrastructure – minimizing integration overhead and business disruption.

Interledger is not necessarily limited to linking bank systems. We envision payments between digital assets/cryptocurrencies and e-wallet services such as those offered by PayPal and Alipay. We are now focusing on interbank payments (in particular, cross-border and cross-currency transactions). Our main source of income is software license fees from financial institutions. For institutions interest in non-fiat payments, the digital asset, XRP, can be used as a bridge currency, via Ripple on-demand liquidity solution, xRapid.

YK: What are the distinguishing features of the business environment?

TO: Current worldwide payments, particularly those that involve international banks, are done via SWIFT (Society for Worldwide Interbank Financial Telecommunication), but in addition to being pre-Internet technology, it is oriented exclusively toward large batch processing and it cannot handle growing needs accompanying changes in global commerce. In fact, current international payments require at least two days on average to complete and about 4% fail.

           It is said that this is because, in the case of overseas remittances, a SWIFT message is sent from the sending bank to the receiving bank, but actual funds are paid between the accounts of the banks. In other words, there are situations when it takes time to complete the remittance and funds are not immediately deposited into the recipient's account. Furthermore, if there is no international payment agreement (correspondent agreement) between the banks, it is possible to send funds through an intermediary bank (correspondent bank). Additionally, there are situations when it takes several days for the intermediary bank to process the transaction. At the same time, there are additional situations when the remittance fee increases.

           Until now, the primary types of international remittances were those between major corporations or financial institutions, and the preceding problem was not evident in abundance. However, because of economic globalization, cross-border EC, and so on, there is greater demand for frequent, small-value international payments. Furthermore, in the era of the smartphone, transactions must be done in real time. Ripple is developing blockchain technologies designed to meet these needs.

YK: Tell us how the business is progressing.

TO: Of the more than 50 top global banks, 15 are participating in or have announced their participation in the Ripple payment network, and more than 75 banks have completed a verification test. Many of the blockchain-technologies are still in the proof-of-concept (PoC) phase, but Ripple's payment solution is already being used for actual fund transfers between real financial institutions.[9]

YK: Tell us about your customers and business partners.

TO: Seven banks that use Ripple–primarily European and US-based banks–formed the Global Payments Steering Group (GPSG), and

---

[9] Example of a remittance between Canada-based ATB Finance and German-based RiseBank. (https://ripple.com/collateral/)

work has begun to standardize procedures and arrangements for overseas remittances using Ripple.

This service provides a lot of freedom on the systems side, but in order to proceed, each bank must execute agreements and put in place remittance procedures. GPSG is working to smooth the process for participating user banks and thereby allow them to begin sending money using Ripple–under standardized, efficient procedures and protocols. It is expected that this standardization will increase the efficiency of remittance operations that use Ripple.

Furthermore, in August 2016, Ripple and SBI Holdings announced the creation of The Japan Bank Consortium. At the point of launch, there were 42 participating banks. The number grew to 61 by July 2017.

YK: Tell us about partnerships and collaborations with financial institutions.

TO: Our working consortium is focused upon the integration of international foreign and domestic exchange, where cutting-edge technology such as blockchain is used, but it is has not been fully institutionalized. The ultimate objective is to realize truly efficient payments across the entire financial superstructure. The intended beneficiaries are participating banks and their customers. Ideally, these banks will reap the benefits of cutting-edge systems, and pass them along to customers in the form of convenience.

The fact of the matter is that many aspects of blockchain technology have reached only the verification stage. When they are actually put to use, everyone will benefit. In particular, the goal of the consortium is to "unify domestic and international exchange" (as indicated in its name) and realize "real-time payments 24-hours a day." Furthermore, the goal is not simply to improve the spread for banks by reducing remittance costs through cutting-edge technology, but also to use it to revise fees for minor payments of 1,000 yen or less, and develop new markets in fields where payments are usually made in cash.

In particular, the consortium has plans to utilize the Ripple technical infrastructure to build and bring to market a private platform referred to as RC Cloud. At first, banks have to introduce the communication software Ripple Connect to make use of xCurrent. The latter simplifies the work of making the process visible, reduces remittance costs, and shortens transaction time, all by eliminating intermediaries in favor of banks directly conducting transactions. Unlike European and US banks that have already moved forward with open development, there are concerns that for Japanese banks, which primarily use mainframe computers, it will be an expensive and time-consuming conversion. In order to reduce the burden, the consortium is endeavoring to establish a unified system.

Furthermore, the consortium is planning to realize real-time payments between banks 24 hours a day, in the very near future. The approach will not only handle foreign exchange transactions provided originally by Ripple, but will also integrate various operations, including domestic exchange. Remittances using Ripple are basically made using the process of banks directly sending receiving money between themselves (Figure 4.12).

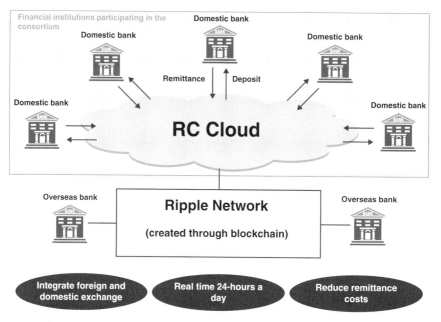

FIGURE 4.12 Ripple Consortium
Source: SBI Ripple Asia.

The recent success of the Japan Bank Consortium is illustrated by the forthcoming release of a groundbreaking smartphone application called "MoneyTap" – powered by Ripple's blockchain technology – to allow customers of the bank consortium to settle transactions instantly, 24 hours a day, seven days a week. "MoneyTap" is the first mobile app of its kind to be developed and used by multiple, different banks in the country.

Three members of the Japan bank consortium: SBI Sumishin Net Bank, Suruga Bank and Resona Bank will be the first to go live on the mobile app in autumn of 2018. This will be followed by a staggered roll out to the rest of consortium.

As indicated in Figure 4.13, both the sending and receiving connect their in-house back-end system to xCurrent, establish a system to remit money, and remit the money using the following procedures:

1. Remitting bank sends a request (remittance amount, receiving bank, name of recipient, bank account number, etc.)

    In contrast with the SWIFT system, the process begins not with remitting the money, but with Ripple-based exchange of remittance information.

2. Because xCurrent connects the sending and receiving bank, all pertinent customer information elements, bank fees, and required time are exchanged and tentatively finalized using xCurrent.

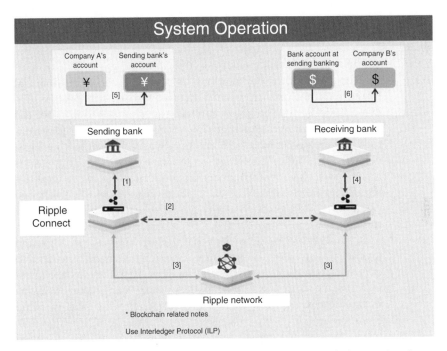

FIGURE 4.13 Diagram of Remitting Money over Ripple Network (Operating the System)
Source: SBI Ripple Asia.

3. Validator confirms transaction information.
4. Funds are transferred according to information confirmed by the banks.

5. When the transaction is finalized, the sending bank transfers funds from the account of its customer (Company A) to the sending bank's account (processed as an intrabank transfer).
6. Similarly, the receiving bank transfers funds from the account of the sending bank to the account of Company B, the recipient.

This example assumes the sending bank has funds in its account at the receiving bank (a remittance method that uses a corresponding bank as before), but Ripple can also handle situations when there is a desire not to conduct the remittance using a nostro (payment) account, which is one of the distinguishing features of the service. In other words, the method makes use of liquidity provided by a third party.

For this construct to be effective, the liquidity provider must have accounts at both banks and can then specify an exchange rate and fee, and also supply liquidity.

YK: Tell us what you will focus on in the future.
TO: Our goal is to provide solutions to problems faced by financial institutions not only in Japan, but also throughout Asia. As discussed, Ripple was originally built as a mechanism to improve the efficiency of foreign exchange operations, and when the joint venture was created in May 2016, the plan was to launch the business, centered on foreign exchange, in Japan. However, during various actual discussions with financial institutions, there were inquiries regarding the possibility of its application for domestic exchange operations. This, as much as anything else, catalyzed the establishment of the consortium.

It immediately became clear that the answer was *yes*. Although Ripple is focused on cross-boarder payment, it can also be used to conduct domestic-transactions, as long as the payments are made in the same currency (e.g., Japanese banks can make payments in Japanese yen). Even so, when discussions were held with the headquarters of US-based Ripple, the response was, "It is possible, but is there really demand for it?" That is because in the United States, there is the ACH system, and domestic interbank payments are highly convenient and inexpensive, so there was little awareness of the issue of domestic exchange outside the United States.

At that time, I too was unsure of the demand for the service, and I had the impression that there were major obstacles to actually putting the system into production. Discussions with numerous banks, however, suggested that all felt there are problems with the current domestic exchange system. This convinced me of the demand potential for the utilization of blockchain technologies in domestic exchange.

Our observations are that countries throughout Asia probably face the same issue. In particular, in developing countries such as Myanmar, there are situations when the lack of banking infrastructure creates a bottleneck for economic development.

Invigorating the financial industry will bring benefits across the entire economy. Throughout Asia, including Japan, providing the option to use cutting-edge financial solutions and contributing to the formation of healthy markets is a challenge that is worth confronting.

Blockchain

R3
Representative: David Rutter, CEO
Company profile
  Founded: 2014
  Clients: Over 200 banks, financial institutions, regulators, trade associations, professional services firms, and technology companies
On November 31, 2016, R3 released the blockchain platform called Corda. The company will develop applications that operate on that platform, in partnership with third parties, and create a financial transaction dedicated ecosystem.

Yoshitaka Kitao: Tell us about your business.
David Rutter: We are currently developing and introducing Corda, an enterprise blockchain platform, which R3 believes will have broad application, specifically for regulated financial institutions, but also across many other sectors of commerce.

Upon considering the risks and relative fragilities that characterize the modern financial system, it's clear that collaboration, again, is the key to achieving the desired end-state for the industry.

A number of technology firms had attempted to build a financial infrastructure reusing some kind of cryptocurrency, but we do not believe the conventional cryptocurrency notion of tokenization is essential to the goal of creating a shared and consistent transaction-execution environment in a capital markets context.

Further, many vendors and startups across the distributed ledger space aspire to tackle only one aspect of the structure or aspire to work as sandboxing software for institutions. These types of single-layer solutions may ultimately create more pain than value, by forging fiefdoms under which organizations must try on a new approach for every different application.

In other words, fit-for-purpose enterprise-grade technology required building a platform from scratch, and not from cloning and idiosyncratically combining existing technologies.

Redundant Record Maintenance Costs

YK: What are the distinguishing features of the business environment?
DR: According to a recent McKinsey study, at the present time, financial firms collectively spend approximately $2.6 trillion on operating costs and 15%–20% of their total expenditures on IT spending.

Large component of these outlays, amounting to billions of dollars annually, involve the cost of reconciling different databases. These expenses may have been sustainable prior to the 2007–2008 financial crisis, but given declining revenues for many financial institutions since the crash, these stubbornly high costs are much harder for banks to bear. The fragmented systems are problematic in many different ways. Particularly burdensome are confirmation and validation delays, expensive maintenance of legacy systems and reconciliation approaches, and inefficient regulatory reporting processes.

Currently, sufficient trust between banks exists to allow for credit extension and credit-based transactions flow, but not enough to enable the sharing and maintenance of internal books and records. As a result, when different firms interact, there are often disparate local and siloed versions of the same information. Maintenance of these separate records is costly for each institution and the expense burden across the entire financial industry is enormous.

Sharing Using Distributed Ledger Technology

DR: In 2014 and 2015, banks faced myriad issues beyond cost management, including declining return on equity, growing competition and demand from customers to improve their technologies and services.

As a result, major financial institutions began to commit more resources to financial innovation teams, some of which were specifically focused on distributed ledger technology. The financial services industry is joined by sectors such as insurance and healthcare in allocating additional resources to exploring this new technology.

But what exactly is new about this technology? First, distributed ledger technology is appealing to financial institutions because it allows disparate systems run by different firms that cannot interact on the basis of unilateral trust to come to an agreement on the existence, nature, and evolution of shared facts and data.

More specifically, financial institutions can review data and know that the different parties that also have access are looking at the same information. This data can be trusted as being reliable without having to create a centralized institution or database. Reliable information is shared for the benefit of each relevant institution and other stakeholding fiduciaries such as regulators. For example, trading counterparties can receive identical source-document information.

With distributed ledgers, the information between institutions is already reconciled. Instant access to a single record can also reduce systemic counterparty and security risk, and foster improvements in reconciliation and regulatory reporting.

Participation in this network of custom versions of systems that all do the same thing, under a shared approach, can create value in areas that have historically afforded institutions little competitive advantage.

Functions That Increase Efficiency

DR: One simplified way of visualizing a distributed ledger is to think of it as a secured spreadsheet that sits in the cloud that multiple parties can edit collaboratively, without concerns as to how other users will access, manipulate, and apply the data. Cryptography ensures authentication for each transaction, guaranteeing that the data's integrity is preserved. Further, the data has an audit trail. Because of their design and features, distributed ledger technologies can ease the burden of the increasing regulatory scrutiny that systemically important financial institutions face (Figure 4.14).

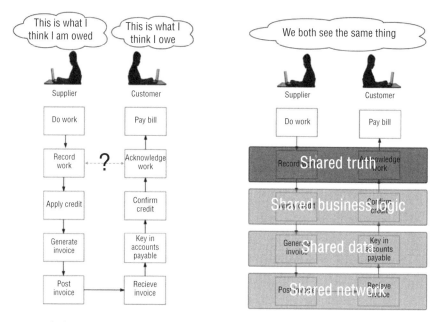

FIGURE 4.14 Sharing Using Distributed-Ledger Technology
Source: R3.

Additionally, smart contracts can direct automatic execution of business logic when certain criteria are met, and allow for the evolution of deal terms according to rules determined by the participants. Some of these advantages could be applied to improve (among many other functions) FX settlement, loan settlement, trade reconciliation, OTC derivatives clearing, cross-border payments, and collateral management.

As a result, the potential system can generate efficiency gains not just for banks but also across the span of financial transactors (e.g., buyer, seller, custodian, registrar, broker, clearer, and regulator). Each of these types of entities stands to benefit from access to a definitive, shared, single record that facilitates their necessary functions. Further, the applications expand well beyond the financial sector because many firms are discovering by launching innovation teams that are trying to adapt distributed ledger technologies.

Given the broad range of entities in the financial system, it is the network features that bestow the greatest benefits associated with distributed ledger technology.

Success of the initiative requires buy-in across the industry for the network effect to bring improvements system-wide. R3 recognized that a broad, cooperative, consortium approach was necessary for the growth and potential of this technology.

In order to achieve this, R3 launched its consortium in early September 2015 with 9 institutions, and by November of that year, 42 had joined in 15 countries. Now, the number of members exceeds 100, including exchanges, buy-side, and insurance companies. Through the consortium, traditional competitors are endeavoring to collaborate in order to reduce their cost base in non strategic areas of business that don't typically offer much room for differentiation. These include settlement, clearing, and back-office processes.

Complaints Regarding Existing Distributed Ledger Technology

DR: The R3 consortium formed an Architecture Working Group to establish the correct architecture for distributed ledgers, and this group quickly recognized that existing distributed ledger technologies did not target the needs of regulated financial institutions. Two requirements – confidentiality and scalability – stood out in particular. The R3 team worked to address the collective needs of the global financial community from a requirements-driven perspective in a series of workshops with senior architects across the consortium. Bitcoin created a technological breakthrough in distributed ledgers, but it features a narrow use case as a means of censorship-resistance cash, and the un permissioned nature of the network and pseudonymous participation presents problems for firms in the regulated financial ecosystem.

By contrast, regulated institutions need a distributed ledger platform built with the existing legal system in mind. Ethereum features another groundbreaking public distributed ledger, but again, it was not built for private interactions between firms, and in its current form is a transparency engine where all parties see all transactions.

Corda, a Distributed Ledger for Managing Financial Transactions

YK: Tell us how the business is progressing.
DR: R3 recognized that an absence of an underlying network and protocol meant that there would be no mechanisms to normalize trading partner assertions or forge authority with them. There are only so many efficiencies to be gained by a ledger that can represent only internal applications or one-off trade agreements.

As a result of the foregoing, in late 2016, we established and open-sourced Corda, a blockchain platform designed to record, manage, and automate legal agreements between business partners. Corda is specifically designed for managing financial agreements between known, identified parties. It differs from traditional public blockchains in that there is not necessarily one single database shared among all participant blocks in a chain (as opposed to Bitcoin and Ethereum, whose cryptocurrencies have blockchains containing records of all data). Corda is a special case of a blockchain that joins data across businesses, with a particular focus on the interaction between computer code and legal documentation. It enforces a system of rules that describe how data involving multiple counterparties should be shared, evolved, validated, and ultimately relied on. Some of Corda's features include the following:

- Recording and managing the evolution of financial agreements and other shared data between two or more identifiable parties in a way that is grounded in existing legal constructs and is compatible with existing regulation
- Validating transactions solely between the direct parties and restricting access to the data within an agreement to only those explicitly entitled or logically privileged to it
- Supporting the inclusion of regulatory and supervisory observer nodes
- Choreographing work flow between firms without a central controller

R3's approach involves using this global protocol for transactions (Corda) alongside a development kit in order to create applications for this protocol (CorDapps). Third parties are encouraged to build user-facing apps, to be available in mobile app stores, on top of the base layer of Corda, for a broad range of different use cases. R3 is working to build a rich developer community, to take advantage of Corda's inbuilt rules, protocols and functions.

The CorDapp model facilitates inclusion of new vendor solutions and in some respects catalyzes a new market for solutions leveraging distributed ledger technology. An orientation of inclusivity and dynamism strongly differentiates R3 from other FinTech companies selling full stack solutions because they must build networks piecemeal in order to sell a particular product.

YK: Tell us what you will focus on in the future.

DR: One major challenge for R3's members is that they cannot build blockchain solutions and take advantage of the fundamental peer-to-peer paradigm in isolation of the broader community. The technology demands consistent collaboration and an openness that has not been a strong point of the financial services industry over the past several decades.

Our members benefit from involvement in collaborative projects that address mutual pain points, thought-leading research works, and regulatory outreach.

The ultimate goal of these projects is to facilitate–through deep collaboration among incumbents, innovators, and regulators–the development of products that will transform the financial services industry and customer experience for the next 20 years.

In our end-state vision, banks, other regulated financial institutions, and other firms are connected to a global network through which they transact, record, and manage their financial agreements with peers, competitors, and counterparties. Here, they would ideally use a suite of certified and interoperable CorDapps, blockchain applications provided by a range of third-party providers, designed to solve specific business issues and that integrate with each firm's own secure registry.

Over time, the R3 team envisions that an increasing amount of nondifferentiating back-office processing will migrate to this platform.

Further, R3 hopes that many legacy systems and approaches will be reevaluated and reconsidered, and that new financial infrastructures will emerge. The focus is on exploring and developing revolutionary technologies that will serve as the new standard for the next 10 to 30 years of financial services (Figure 4.15).

On May 23, 2017, R3 completed its first two of three rounds of series-A financing. The company raised more than $100 million from over 40 companies in 15 countries. The investment roster includes the SBI Group, Bank of America, Merrill Lynch, HSBC, Intel, and Temasek. This was the world's largest investment sequence mapped to a company involved in DLT and blockchain technology.

R3 will use these funds to accelerate its development of technology and introduce products through strategic partnerships. The company plans to focus its energy primarily on Corda, a blockchain platform for businesses and infrastructure network, that support enterprise-grade applications that seamlessly operate with existing systems and networks created by numerous partners.

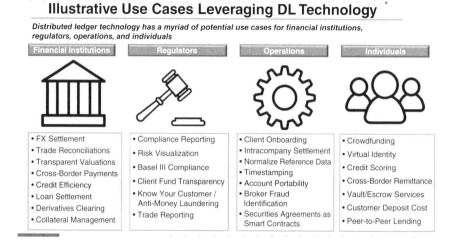

Illustrative Use Cases Leveraging DL Technology

Distributed ledger technology has a myriad of potential use cases for financial institutions, regulators, operations, and individuals

Financial Institutions	Regulators	Operations	Individuals

• FX Settlement
• Trade Reconciliations
• Transparent Valuations
• Cross-Border Payments
• Credit Efficiency
• Loan Settlement
• Derivatives Clearing
• Collateral Management
	• Compliance Reporting
	• Risk Visualization
	• Basel III Compliance
	• Client Fund Transparency
	• Know Your Customer /
	  Anti-Money Laundering
	• Trade Reporting
		• Client Onboarding
		• Intracompany Settlement
		• Normalize Reference Data
		• Timestamping
		• Account Portability
		• Broker Fraud
		  Identification
		• Securities Agreements as
		  Smart Contracts
			• Crowdfunding
			• Virtual Identity
			• Credit Scoring
			• Cross-Border Remittance
			• Vault/Escrow Services
			• Customer Deposit Cost
			• Peer-to-Peer Lending

FIGURE 4.15 Situations Where Distributed Ledger Technology Plays an Active Role
Source: R3.

Big Data

Treasure Data
  Representative: Hiro Yoshikawa, Founder and CEO
  Company profile
    Founded: 2011
    Number of customers: 300 companies
    Example clients: Pioneer Corporation, Dentsu, Shiseido
  Treasure Data provides Treasure CDP Customer Data Platform. The goal is to connect vertically segregated data, enabling the smooth and easy use of this information as a business tool.

Yoshitaka Kitao: Tell us about the history of the company.
Hiro Yoshikawa: Treasure Data is a Silicon Valley-based startup company established by three Japanese individuals (me, Kazuki Ota, and Sada Furuhashi) in December 2011. One year later, the company opened an office in Japan and, in 2015, we set up third office in Korea.

We provide a cloud based Data Management Solution and Customer Data Platform, Treasure CDP, which links vertically segmented data in such a way as to enable instantaneous use by our customers. Treasure CDP is used by about 300 companies throughout the world, as part of their digital transformation, including IoT and digital marketing. The system can handle vast amounts of divergent unstructured data types, including web-viewing patterns and data logs from various applications and mobile devices. Our system facilitates the collection, storage, analysis, and connection to other marketing tools – all for a set yearly fee. Furthermore, we are working on projects ranging from sensor- and machine-generated data processing to reinforce our big data presence in the IoT field.

YK: Tell us about your business.
HY: The service is applicable across various areas of the economy, including finance-related applications and data generated from various sources, including ads, Internet activity, and mobile app usage. Our clients are digital business players, primarily major companies.

Our service is geared toward major companies seeking to compete against disruptive companies, particularly in the areas of B2C and B2B2C companies, which are also important customers.

The business employs a fixed, yearly fee with no upfront expenditures – a so-called platform as a service (PaaS) – fee model. The rate structure begins at several millions of yen a month, depending on the volume of data and calculation resources required to analyze customer issues.

YK: What are the distinguishing features of the business environment?
HY: The following three technologies have evolved and spread dramatically, and the services that Treasure Data provides are extremely important for participants in the areas described here.

The first is sensors. Nowadays the word IoT is picked up in the news every day. With countless connected devices spread throughout the world (particularly in final products), companies can identify the location and specific nature of product use, whether products are operating correctly, and when they might break down.

Second is the importance of network structures. With the spread of the Internet and then mobile services, Wi-Fi, LPWA (low-power wide-area), and other network structures, it has become possible for sensors to monitor consumer behavior with remarkable accuracy. The potential applications associated with the ubiquitous spread of smartphones alone are virtually limitless.

The third is the emergence of the cloud. Cloud technology, which separates the physical server from the logical application, has also made it possible to transform business ideas into actual services at very low cost. We are able to handle big data quickly and cheaply by using the cloud.

As these three technical verticals advance, it will become possible to ascertain the buying and use behavior of consumers in ways that were unknown before. In addition, there has been dramatic growth in the volume of log data generated from sensors, mobile apps, and cloud services. These instances continue to increase.

The sheer volume of log data has grown so explosively that it has become is impossible to transform it into valuable information with existing technology. Therefore, we decided to create our own database from scratch and link it to networks on a cloud-based platform. It was possible to receive log data because it can be used in digital business. One could say that services caught up with peripheral technology (Figure 4.16).

YK: Tell us how the business is progressing.
HY: Over the past several years, the number of data elements provided by the 300 companies that use the Treasure Data services have grown to 120 trillion. The service collects about one million data units per second.

YK: Tell us about your customers and business partners.
HY: I would like to discuss an example in the FinTech field that integrates IoT and big data. On June 22, 2015, Pioneer Corporation announced a partnership in its telematics services business with Insurance Company. Pioneer, a recognized brand as a global manufacturer of audio equipment and car navigation systems, launched a telematics business for car insurance.[10]

In order to achieve its objectives, in 2006, Pioneer built a proprietary network system that makes use of probe information (data obtained from cars when they are in operation), and the company is now seeking to establish itself as an innovator in the use of big data. In 2014, they established a partnership with us, and together we have been accumulating knowledge as to the best uses of big data in the field of transportation.[11]

This business, which Pioneer and Insurance Company are undertaking in collaboration, has the object of improving vehicle safety operation support. In September 2014, we established a partnership with Pioneer on this business to provide big data technology and services.

[10] Pioneer Corporation news release, http://pioneer.jp/corp/news/press/2015/pdf/0622-1.pdf.

[11] Pioneer Corporation news release, http://pioneer.jp/corp/news/press/2014/pdf/0904-2.pdf.

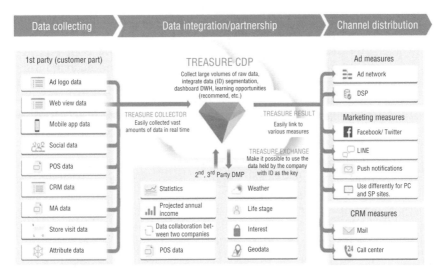

FIGURE 4.16 Digital Marketing Using Treasure CDP
Source: Treasure Data

This is a prime example of the insurance industry collaborating on technology and using services from a different industry as a means of launching new financial services.

We expect this business to grow, particularly as more data is collected from vehicles. We believe we are well-positioned to facilitate increases in the precision of driving evaluations. If so, it will enhance the safety of the transportation system and the peace of mind associated with vehicular travel.

We hope to use our data platform and their data to analyze the driving patterns of individuals in order to personalize the calculation of premiums and, in doing so, to lower premiums for safe drivers.

YK: Tell us about partnerships and collaborations with financial institutions.

HY: In addition to telematic insurance programs just discussed, there are numerous cases in which technology will make it possible to increase the range and sophistication levels of financial services. Centralized exchanges and remittance networks will become less important because it has become possible to securely exchange information through P2P, making use of blockchain, and so on, and, by doing so, reduce the cost of remitting to previously unheard of levels. We also envision the enhanced ability for entities to raise small amounts of money at lower costs, by doing so over the web.

We are introducing every service we offer on both the web and smartphones, and our applications create and maintain a log for each action. In addition to improving reliability, the logs can be used to analyze the tastes and preferences of users in a digital marketing trend. In turn, companies can use the results to drive product design, screening operations, credit decisions, and promotions of the most appropriate product offerings.

Given the big data environment and infrastructure we have created, we also believe it feasible to analyze social media as a means of assessing consumer attitudes and to capture commercial opportunities accordingly. Turning to the field of insurance, the basic reason that consumers purchase it is in case of an emergency, but there will also probably be advances in preventing emergencies, illnesses, and accidents through the use of algorithms and data.

YK: Tell us what you will focus on in the future.

HY: Treasure Data will now start turning its attention to the field of data management solution. Data management solution refers to companies and applications making free use of all the various types of vertically segmented data by linking them in order to create business successes as discussed. Finance has traditionally been well suited for the use of data and technology. We want to expand our business to promote the use of data within companies, among companies, and between industries in order to get consumers to use various other convenient services.

YK: What is the future outlook?

HY: Digital disrupters such as Google, Facebook, Netflix, and Uber are steadily making use of data and technology to revolutionize businesses. In turn, this is causing other entities to focus on rediscovering their own strengths. They are endeavoring to use platforms like ours to generate new disruptions.

Technologies such as blockchains are likely to make exchanged information itself reliable, eliminate cash, and drive expenditures for services such as foreign exchange and remittances to almost zero. Financial transactions will have the look and feel of sending an email or LINE message. Activities such as credit screening will probably be done using personalized data, such as activity logs, without the constraints of uniform rules. They will be made instantaneously.

It is my opinion that in the future, it will be possible to flexibly launch businesses with even less capital, and that for expenditures, savings and investments, users will be able to select better options.

To summarize, consumers of the future will, for the first time, have access to financial tools similar to those used by large companies and institutions. It is our intention to position Treasure Data's services as a driver of these improvements.

Big Data

GiXo Ltd.
   Representative: Tomohiro Amino, Director and CEO
   Company profile
   Founded: 2012
   Number of customers: 30 companies
   Example customers: beverage manufacturer, department store, credit card company, general home electronics manufacturer, general machine manufacturer, restaurant chain, city bank, regional bank, etc.
   GiXo provides services that integrate big data analysis and strategic consulting. The company possesses strengths in various fields, including utilizing analytics and big data to reinforce the competitiveness of companies from a business strategy perspective.

Yoshitaka Kitao: Tell us about the history of the company.
Tomohiro Amino: I will begin with a summary of my background in order to introduce our business model.

   After working on planning at a private company, I moved to the consulting firm Accenture. For about seven years I worked in a department that offered strategic consulting, and I was involved in numerous projects related to proposing new businesses using customer purchase data and behavior data. This was a time when the terms *big data* and *IoT* were unknown. We analyzed data possessed by clients, transformed that data into information, and used that information to develop opinions designed to enhance the competitiveness of client companies or to facilitate the launch of new businesses. While I was deeply involved with these efforts, I was fascinated by the possibilities of large volumes of data and its analysis.

   After Accenture, I moved to IBM Japan's Business Analytics and Optimization (BAO), an organization that supports efforts by clients to strengthen their competitiveness using big data and analytics. At BAO, my mission was to extol the value of big data that companies possess and to offer suggestions as to how best to use this data in order to get client companies to introduce hardware and software.

I performed this service for many clients, and as I discussed issues with managers, I formed one strong idea: Top management needs information derived from inputs and opinions based on an interpretation of the results of data analysis. Companies spend vast resources to get this information, and I didn't believe that these resources were, in all cases, allocated efficiently.

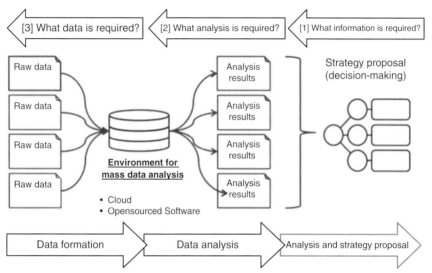

FIGURE 4.17 Consulting Based on the Receipt of a Large Volume of Data
Source: GiXo Ltd.

A comment by one manager really stuck with me. "Mr. Amino, it will take one year to create the system, one year to train the personnel, and one year to generate results. During that time, I will be fired by shareholders."

That was just around the time that cloud services and open source services appeared, and an era where massive investments would not be necessary to analyze large volumes of data was approaching. Furthermore, there began to be an extensive availability of open source languages and tools suitable for statistics and analysis, such as R and Python, and it was no longer necessary to introduce expensive software for these purposes. It quickly became possible to implement "a service model for obtaining large volumes of data from clients, analyzing that data oneself, and then proposing marketing measures and business strategy by interpreting those results" (Figure 4.17).

Working with my former IBM Japan colleagues, we launched GiXo, whose name incorporates the following idea: "The world is really keen on the buzzword big data, but analysis of vast volumes of data without thinking about results is garbage output." An old saying about databases is "garbage in, garbage out." and just like that, society's dreams may end in disappointment. Even data content that looks like a mountain of garbage at first glance can probably be rendered useful if a thoughtful person conducts analysis, and interprets the results. Let's prove that to society. Let's achieve "garbage in, something valuable out."

YK: Tell us how the business is progressing.

TA: When the company was founded, we launched a program called Team CMO. This is a service for top management that replaces or supports the chief marketing officer (CMO). Fortunately, we were blessed with clients and the business had a relatively smooth start.

A success example that I can discuss is View Card, a credit card subsidiary within the JR East Japan Group. The objective of the View Card initiative was to analyze information possessed by the company (e.g., membership data), develop a marketing strategy based on the results of that analysis, and promote new membership and use on an informed, data-driven basis.

One of the company's products is the View Suica card. It is the only credit card that can automatically charge the contactless fare card Suica, and users can earn triple points when charging their Suica card. This auto-charge function is convenient and a deal, and this can be used to appeal to customers.

An analysis of auto-charge transaction patterns revealed a high rate of usage, and low incidence of termination. In turn, this reinforced the value proposition embedded in the auto-charge function. Based on this intelligence, management made the bold decision to thoroughly base appeals, including ads and taglines, on the auto-charger function, which generated the largest monthly increase in new members in history. In response to this success, a data and analytics culture took root in the company, which continues its efforts to implement data-driven marketing and data-driven management.

As the project has progressed, the scope of the data we handle has grown. The company possesses more than 10 years of historical payment information, and other data related to various types of factors, such as web members and web detailed use, was added. The breadth, volume, and frequency of data has grown to include various types of data that only train companies possess, such as history of where riders get on and off special express trains, their use of accumulated points, and their participation in special campaigns.

When GiXo was established, it had a strong feel of a marketing consulting firm that could process large volumes of data, but about 18 months after the company was established, it had reached a level where it could handle large volumes of data for strategic proposals, and we were not embarrassed to call ourselves a company that provides big data service.

Using Technology and Generating Value Added

YA: The breadth and volume of incoming data increased and a wider range of items could be analyzed, which caused a dramatic increase in the workloads of Team CMO's analysis team.

The Measures Proposal Team, a subgroup of Team CMO, interprets the results of the perpetual analysis of a proposed hypothesis, and reverts to the Analysis Team to conduct tests to verify new ideas. For the View Card project, one new topic after another comes up because the marketing meeting when reports are made to top management, is held every other week.

The Analysis Team must conduct reviews of the continually increasing types and volume of data. There are also frequent changes in the priority of what is to be analyzed. It goes without saying that the work of rivals is also progressing. We increased the number of new employees to handle the growing operations, but various mistakes occurred because the implicit data analysis process was not properly processed, and this increased the operational burden. A vicious cycle developed at the workplace.

Mr. Hanatani, who is responsible for the Analysis Team, felt that the company would fail if things continued in that way, and he took the lead in responding to this challenge. What should be done to ensure precise analysis without mistakes even among new members? How should the data be stored as analysis infrastructure? What type of analysis system should there be? What type of analytical framework should be built? Who should be put in charge of how much? How should the scope of roles and responsibilities be set? Data analysis is just a method. How should we focus on interpreting analysis results in order to generate added value? In response to these questions, we have worked to achieve both advanced, high-quality analysis and productivity, and constructed an analysis system that only GiXo could provide (Figure 4.18). We patented this analysis system and process, and this has become the key to maintaining our competitiveness.

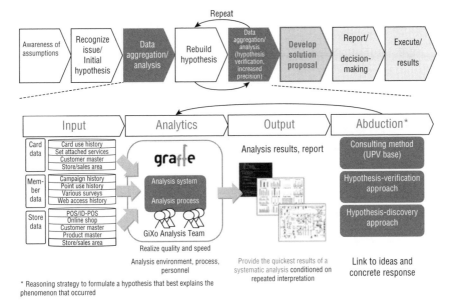

FIGURE 4.18 GiXo Service Model
Source: GiXo Ltd.

Increase in "Amount of Thinking" in the World

In February 2016, we increased our capital base through a third-party allotment from SBI Investment, and used the opportunity to rework our vision, mission and value proposition. At that time, our operations were in satisfactory shape, but we saw the capital injection as catalyst for incremental optimization. Most importantly, we asked ourselves how we could put the money to best use.

Data analysis is our core service, and it is our opinion that data analysis is indispensable for more sophisticated planning operations. However, in planning operations, analysis is considered trivial work that managers often seek to eliminate.

For planning operations, action and execution are the most important factors. We thoroughly considered what should be done to maximize the thinking time for people working on planning–that is, what should be done to develop a concrete response in the shortest time.

When the company was founded, we thought it is a waste for clients to invest in new systems and hire personnel to conduct analysis, and our belief in this premise is even stronger now.

Therefore, we redefined our vision; we would increase the amount of thinking in the world. We believed that the best means of achieving that objective was to thoroughly investigate the speed and quality of our analytics.

Many companies allocate business resources to R&D, and Mr. Tanaka, who is a responsible for the company's strategy, and decided whether the allocation is consistent with this mission and vision, approved the allocation. About 40% of GiXo employees work exclusively in the R&D field, and we are thoroughly investigating speed and quality of analytics. A lot of R&D efforts end in failure, but we have begun to see several seeds that have outstanding future potential.

Payment Data Shows the Character of Consumers

YK: Tell us what you will focus on in the future.
YA: From my perspective, it appears that technology to make payments convenient and economical – that is, FinTech – will be the driving force of our growth. Our work in the FinTech field is related to making use of payment data, and I cannot deny that being called a FinTech company makes me a bit uncomfortable, but I will explain our efforts.

We consider payment data extremely valuable. This is because it reveals the character of consumers, including the nature of their relationships with stores.

When asked how do you define grade-A customers? Many companies answer by giving a threshold value for annual frequency of use. Few define grade-A customers in terms of how they want customers to use their products and services – that is, customers who make good use of the company. With respect to our retail efforts as an example, grade-A customers are defined in terms of how they purchase and use the company's products and services, not simply in terms of the money they spend.

Furthermore, let's look at the credit card industry. Many companies define a grade-A customer as one that makes 600,000 to 1,000,000 yen or more in purchases per year. Few companies respond by saying how grade-A customers use their credit cards. When companies define purchase behavior of ideal customers for their company, they consider how much customers purchase with their cards per year. Annual purchases are probably a fine resulting indicator attached afterward when centered on purchase behavior.

It is now possible to answer the previous question by creating a single map that enables companies to ascertain current customer purchase patterns and profitability with a single chart, and to use that map to identify the customers upon which the company should focus in order to grow the business.

In order to create that map, we are developing an algorithm to divide users into 15 groupings, and to monitor the percentage of users, amount of use, and number of use categories for each segment. In addition, the system monitors the payment methodologies of each customer, and determines consumer spending trends – equivalent to the wallet share used at each merchant (category of facility). The creation of that map is automated with the inflow of credit card transaction data.

Owing to this, it is possible to ascertain the current condition of client companies in detail, and focus solely on the customer development methods will best grow the business. In other words, we will maximize thinking time.

Algorithms for main favorable trend and consumer spending trend will be adapted for B2C companies, such as retailers, and it will be possible to apply them if there is data on customer purchases and use. Furthermore, the technology for estimating wallet size for consumer spending trends can be tied to credit information for business loan service based on accounting transactions.

How to Define a Customer as a Grade-A Customer

YA: I would like to discuss another effort related to payment data. The driving factor of the customer – store relationship is the manner in which the customer chooses to use the store. Understanding how customers in a particular condition will behave is the next priority associated with efforts to increase the quality of the customer for the company. Because there is a desire to put a monetary figure on the grades of customers, and there are qualitatively ascertained changes in these categories, we developed and patented an approach and algorithm to determine the next action based on customer loyalization, which makes use of data such as payment data (Figure 4.19).

For credit cards, we calculate to what extent the grade of the customer's credit card use improves if payment at a particular merchant (category) takes root. We will undertake marketing activities to promote the use by customers, taking into consideration this quantitative information.

For credit cards, compelling the use of automatic withdrawal for bills such as utilities (commonly called recurring payments) is the sure way to establish grade-A customers, but these arrangements are subject to change.

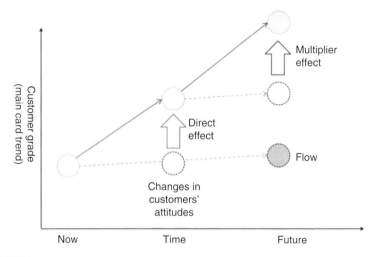

FIGURE 4.19 The Next Action-Based Customer Loyalization Approach
Source: GiXo Ltd.

Converting payment behavior of each individual customer into a monetary amount makes it possible to control the incentives to reflect future value of customers.

If we look at banks as an example, it is possible to make judgments about a person's credit status by estimating the monetary value of the future improvement in the customer's grade, starting with the home loan behavior.

For the retail industry, it is possible to create incentives for consumers. The industry is now beginning to apply financial system tools such as credit sales, advancing points and making it possible to make use of post-payment methods until a certain amount of prepaid card is used. It is possible to apply mechanisms to ascertain to what degree transactions improve the grade of customers of various industries, and this will change how marketing is conducted.

I have discussed fields that fall, at least indirectly, into the general category of FinTech, and this component of our business has overlaps, but is not identical, to our core mission of maximizing time to think. Calculating the economic value from the perspective of the future value of customers generates important inputs to the objective of creating customer strategy: our strength. Our approach covers all 4Ps of marketing (place, price, product, and promotion). We research and develop approaches and calculation methods for understanding customers from a strategy perspective and build up component technologies to capture associated opportunities.

We want to continue to develop services that seek to maximize the thinking time of client companies, thus providing value to our customers, offering consumers better services, and making the world even easier to live in.

AI and Big Data

Generic Solution Corporation
Representative: Ryosuke Konishi, Director, CEO, and CTO
Company profile
Founded: 2006
Partners: Chiba Bank, Chugoku Bank, Daishi Bank, SBI SECURITIES
Generic Solution Corporation provides data mining software and services for businesses that use big data. The company's business intelligence (BI), business analytics (BA), and recommendation tools are differentiated from competitors in that our methods: automate the analysis process, individual customer analysis can be conducted, and the results of the data usage can be checked.

Yoshitaka Kitao: Tell us about the history of the company.

Ryosuke Konishi: Established in May 2006, the business was incorporated and operations were launched in December of the same year. When the business was established, I was researching databases at the Kiyoki Lab of Keio University. With a vision of stressing connections with real society, Professor Yasushi Kiyoki focused on differences between the human memory system and computer processing mechanisms, and he was motivated by the question of whether it is possible to create a database with the ability to evaluate human conditions and tap into memory banks.

Consider, for example, the word *blue*. If one enters this word into normal search engines–including Google–the search algorithm will only return answers containing the word *blue*.

People, however, are different. When one hears *blue* at a street intersection, one thinks of a traffic light (In Japanese, the green traffic light is called *blue*) and interprets it to mean *go*, but if one hears the same word in a room all by oneself, one can interpret it as "being sort of sad." Even for the same word, humans tap their memories, which bring about both direct and indirect associations.

My research topic covered methodologies for creating curricula tailor-made to individual learners, taking into consideration the cause-and-effect and dependency of topics in the fields of education and learning. Our goal was to develop a system to effectively support recommended learning content for individual learners. It would not simply suggest questions similar to ones answered incorrectly but create an individual study curriculum that makes learning easy so that strongly related peripheral topics came next and those that are dependent are studied first.

We received a request from an E-commerce retailer that wanted to use its database to increase per-customer spending (Figure 4.20).

Background for establishing the company and current state of the company

In order to create an intelligent computer, it was necessary to first develop technology to uncover the meaning from data, and we were successful in efficiently processing large volumes of data and applying that data to real society.

⇒ Artificial intelligence refers to technologies that support automation of the PDCA cycle through the autonomous acquisition of knowledge, expression, and learning.

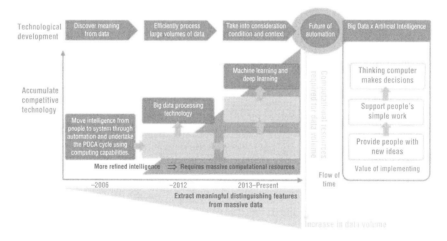

FIGURE 4.20 From Establishment until Now
Source: Generic Solution.

For product recommendations based on collaborative filtering (system to extract correlation of likes), such as those deployed by Amazon, a problem emerges insofar as there are negative customer satisfaction impacts for products that have strong preference characteristics, (i.e., that people either love or hate) such as natto and milk. We developed a system to dynamically display websites for particular individuals. Its purpose is to increase per-customer spending through recommendation of products that are appropriate, given the specific preferences and rhythms identified for individual customers. We worked on the system development for about one year and were able to increase per-customer spending by about 15%. This success became the formative experience of the current company and business.

The company, Generic Solution, is a youth-based organization, centered on its founder, who achieved success as a student entrepreneur. Its engineering team is comprised of university friends and acquaintances, who assisted in the spinout of a major company. Working with these individuals, I formed a highly adaptable expert team, resilient to challenges, and determined to support corporate innovation associated with routine operations.

YK: Tell us about your business.

RK: For the solutions that we provide, there is a strong awareness of our introductory trial-and-error efforts and an actual society that understands the demands of the time. We are focused on working with entities that are committed to creating high customer value and to the delivery of methods for providing services that are easy to adopt.

We have two main businesses. For the analytics business, we consult with clients to create actual automated solutions that individually respond to the demands and expectations of customers. For the solutions business, which is builds upon these successes, we provide data mining and machine-learning software and services, thereby enabling the establishment and realization of goals tied to profits for customers who want to make use of big data. The company's BI/BA and recommendation tools are different than those of its competitors, because we make it possible to automate the analysis of individual customer data use, in a verifiable manner.

YK: What are the distinguishing features of the business environment?

RK: The advent of personal computers has driven various changes in society, and created an environment for generating new value. Subsequently, the information society, in which computers store vast amounts of data and people communicate via the Internet, created new industries and enhanced life experiences. The diffusion of mobile computers is similarly affecting all aspects of consumers' lives.

In an information environment that generates various types of data in real time, technology that supports more sophisticated use of this information, is rapidly evolving. First, big data analysis technology has made it possible to quickly process large volumes of stored information through distributed computing. Next, various startup companies are taking on the challenge of applying artificial intelligence technology to fields, such as ascertaining conditions and understanding context, when it had been technically difficult to do so in the past.

In the future, there will be no computers that require users to read massive manuals to operate, society will be able to make use of information, and computers will possess integrated intelligence. These new machines will not be viewed as devices but rather as embedded in everyday human experience.

Purchaser decision-making that employs advanced technology will lead to dilemmas. When adopting such new technologies, just as for traditional IT systems, purchasers who are not experts will make idiosyncratic demands of vendors, and this will render it difficult for vendors to develop optimal systems. In order to benefit from this new technology, there will be a need for human resources with technical knowledge and skills. It is difficult to recruit and train these individuals. Under these conditions, leaders who are knowledgeable of in-house operations will play an important role, and, in particular, there will be demands for professionals who can play the role of in-house receiver of new technology.

YK: Tell us how the business is progressing.

RK: We are a small organization of about 20 employees, the center of which is our core technology development team. Since the company's formation in 2006, we have consistently worked on building and selling artificial intelligence technology for data mining and machine learning and have developed distributed computing technology to analyze big data. These efforts drive our current business, and we believe that we are attracting the interest of new customers.

We have been fortunate enough to work with customers in various economic segments, including education, logistics, retail, and finance. In the future, we will also undertake efforts in the field of IoT for the manufacturing industry and social infrastructure (Figure 4.21).

	Switch from human intelligence to system intelligence through automation and implement PDCA cycle using computing capabilities.				

	Location of intelligence	Data storage	Data analysis method	Data processing infrastructure	Added value
Existing methods	People	Star schema	Ad-hoc	Scale up	People-based PDCA
	Employee training	High physical performance	Manipulate people's freedom	Need for excess IT resources	Chronic shortage of personnel
	Specialization	Burden on machine	Degree of freedom for data analysis	Machine price	Secure personnel
	Technical skills	High virtual performance	Standard demands	Most appropriate IT resource for demands	Power of team of experts
GS8-based method	System	Dispersed scheme	Fixed	Scale out	System-based PDCA

FIGURE 4.21 Fields Our Product GS8 Is Used In

Source: Generic Solution.

YK: Tell us about partnerships and collaborations with financial institutions.

RK: Financial institutions accumulate important data on topics such as asset formation of customers. Using that information, it is possible to use big data to identify potential financial needs and thereby uncover hidden value. Artificial intelligence can capture even small changes in customer profiles.

Is it possible to detect or generate changes in the financial behavior of individual customers? In order to do so it is likely important to uncover or create the background for the customer's connection to financial products.

Our job is to identify the ideal function of big data, artificial intelligence and FinTech as technologies that financial institutions should adopt, and propose concepts designed to create a foundation for confronting long-term issues while generating short-term successes.

We propose that financial institutions introduce omni channel financial operations by building an environment to make integrated use of data stored on core systems. From there, we believe they should develop systems to support the transformation of information generated through customer interactions, into processable data. Furthermore, there are hopes for linking data both inside and outside the company to treat customers as individuals. In this field, we are examining the utilization of statistical data and its application to the generally available information about individual consumers and corporations.

IT systems of this nature are growing, evolving, and affecting actual society. Furthermore, the success of organizations that make trial use of new technology will support that evolution.

YK: Tell us about your customers and business partners.

RK: One bank implemented data mining targeting individuals in order to promote the use of credit cards based on actual use. Furthermore, for investment trusts and insurance products, the bank ascertained changes in the financial needs of individual customers, and staff were able to efficiently increase the amount of deposited assets by calling on customers with this information in hand. It was also possible to re-approach customers who were covered using traditional methods, and doing so resulted in a 10% increase in the number of customers. Although these individuals were already customers of the bank, they also routinely did business with other financial institutions. Our methods enabled them to capture a greater share of individual customer flows.

Using another bank as an example, we developed a model to forecast the financing needs of individuals – that is, when they will borrow money – from the regularity of deposits and withdrawals and were able to increase uncollateralized business in this manner.

For business-lending companies, however, we conducted an analysis of annual data using financial document data accumulated to date. We are currently developing a system for determining operating capital needs using daily transaction data, such as foreign exchange data, that makes it possible to approach the financial staff of client corporations in a timely manner.

YK: Tell us what you will focus on in the future.

RK: As efforts to transform information into data progresses, it will likely become possible, in various situations, to make use of real-time data. We want to develop technologies that not only capture but also interpret this information for the purposes of incremental business capture.

Until now, we have focused on developing artificial intelligence technology centered on transaction data, but in the future, we would like to work on developing technology that can be applied to the field of robotics, specifically by broadening technical fields to include image analysis, computer vision and verbal communication.

Cloud Accounting

freee

Representative: Daisuke Sasaki, Director and CEO

Company profile

Founded: 2012

Number of customers: 800,000 worksites (offices)

Example partners: Mizuho Bank, Fukuoka Financial Group, Hokkoku Bank, SBI Sumishin Net Bank

The company freee provides cloud accounting software, also called freee (hereinafter called the *accounting Freee*). The product is primarily targeted to small businesses, medium-sized enterprises, and sole proprietorships. The software features numerous functions, including those related to creating financial statements, issuing bills and estimates, managing accounts receivable and payable, and adjusting expenses.

Yoshitaka Kitao: Tell us about the history of the company.

Daisuke Sasaki: With a vision of making it possible for all people involved with small businesses to focus on creative activities, freee has provided, since its creation, an offering of cloud products, centered on the accounting freee offering.

Several formative experiences informed this vision. When I was working as the manager in charge of marketing for small- and medium-sized enterprises in the Asia Pacific region at Google's Japan office, a coworker from the United States visited Japan. He was shocked that the main form of communication between businesses was faxes. At the Smithsonian Museum in the United States, faxes are displayed as an industrial relic. This symbolized how much Japanese small- and medium-sized enterprises and sole proprietorships lagged behind the United States and Europe, in terms of use of technology.

At that time, I remembered accounting operations at a startup company at which I had once served as CFO. There, the accounting staff posted revenues and expenditures and claim and liability data into multiple tools such as Excel sheets, accounting software, Internet banking apps and so on. In addition to accounting, overall back-office operations, including calculating salary and completing administrative procedures, entailed numerous such redundant and inefficient such tasks.

I was convinced that startup companies should be focused solely on business growth, and that increasing the efficiency of extremely inefficient back-office processes would be of great value to society. I thus began to develop the accounting freee, using my apartment as my office.

Automation, Simplification, Optimization

YK: Tell us about your business.

DS: The accounting Freee product has captured the top share of the cloud accounting software market in Japan, with more than 800,000 offices using this software.

The distinguishing features of the software are automation, simplification, and optimization. The accounting freee program acquires data on Internet banking and credit card use, assigns it to accounts using artificial intelligence, and automatically journalizes the output. In addition to this financial institution data, posting and journalizing work is automated by linking to various independent services, such as cloud POS and EC platforms. We acquired two patents as a pioneer in the field of automated journalizing, and we continue to invest in technology through joint research with universities.

In addition, freee not only eliminates the widely used direct digitalization of paper account books but also employs screens that avoid accounting terminology as much as possible. Therefore, even managers with little knowledge of bookkeeping and employees who are not engaged in accounting are able to easily use the software.

Making It Possible to Optimize Overall Accounting Operations

DS: The fact that employees can easily use the accounting freee for issuing invoices at sales offices and for adjusting expenses shows that it is not simply accounting software, but also was designed as a product to optimize overall accounting operations, including accounts receivable and payable management before the accounting treatment, and cash flow management.

Furthermore, freee is not only for accounting operations. With a single account, people can use freee for both accounting and any of a series of cloud services for a wide range of operations, including founding a company, launching businesses, and managing human resources. These services are managed through Company

Founding freee and Launching Businesses freee, which reduce the burden of filing forms when registering a company or launching a sole proprietorship, and HR Management Calculation freee, which increases the efficiency of human resources dynamic. All increase the efficiency of overall back-office operations.

The freee solution is used by businesses of various sizes, of various types, in various stages of development. For example, at Factory, a cafe located in Shibuya, the entry of information when registers are closed each day has been automated by linking the cloud POS to freee. Therefore, accounting operations were transformed from ending the day by entering sales data into the computer to checking the data that has been compiled into a report and using that for business decisions, all of which has been automatically prepared.

Even for medium-sized enterprises, freee is used as a tool to reform operations. Attax Tax Accounting Firm has used freee to improve operations at medium-sized enterprises (i.e., those with about 500 employees). In the past, the management department handled all the data entry operations, but after introducing freee, whom frontline employees can easily use, the company was able to both distribute the workload and conduct management based on almost real-time figures. One of the features, and arguably a major advantage, of using cloud services is that it makes it possible for customer companies to undertake management in close partnership with their accounting firms.

Even startup companies that are endeavoring to go public are availing themselves of freee as an extremely easy-to-use, inexpensive cloud enterprise resource planning (ERP) software that can optimize overall back office operations. It is not uncommon for traditional ERP software to costs tens of millions of yen to introduce and operate, but it is now possible to use such cloud software at an extremely low cost.

Promoting the Spread of Online Banking

YK: Tell us about partnerships and collaborations with financial institutions.

DS: In December 2015, freee announced the freee Financial Institution Advisor Account, which makes it possible for banks to view users' accounting data on a permissioned basis. After that, we announced partnerships with 21 (as of August 2017) financial institutions that range from mega banks to online banking and regional financial institutions (Figure 4.22). The switch to a more

Time	Partner bank	Announcement
May 2016	Japan Net Bank	Introduction of solutions for automated accounts receivable cash application using one-time accounts
July 2016	Tottori Bank	Introduction of Internet banking plan for freee
August 2016	Resona Bank	Sponsorship of Resona Bank's Entrepreneurship Support Pac and introduction of accounting freee at a special price
August 2016	SBI Sumishin Next Bank	Introduction of API to acquire banking statements and began to examine an API for transfers
September 2016	Mizuho Bank	Ability for users to open a corporate account in one step from freee
October 2016	Mizuho Bank	Introduction of API to acquire banking statements
October 2016	Japan Net Bank	Introduction of business loans that make use of accounting freee data.

FIGURE 4.22 Partnership with Financial Institutions
Source: freee.

stable and secure API, from the current web scraping of bank account activity information for Internet banking, the core of accounting automation, will probably have a major impact on users, extending to partnerships with financial institutions.

The first Japanese bank API to acquire account activity information was able to do so through collaboration between freee and SBI Sumishin Net Bank. Working with SBI Sumishin Net Bank, we are also moving forward with a fund transfer API link that makes it possible to complete the process through a natural flow from accounts receivable and payable management operations. This was the first step in the logical migration of all accounting operations to the cloud.

The ability to automate accounting processes in a secure and stable manner will lead to a greater demand for Internet banking. Only about 20% of small- and medium-sized enterprises use this technology, but highlighting the combined benefits of third-party applications such as freee may lead to greater use of Internet banking itself.

Data stored by freee can be used for business loan service based on accounting transactions and generate added value for both users and financial institutions.

Increase the Efficiency of the Financing Process

DS: By automating and increasing the efficiency of back-office operations, freee helps small business focus on core business objectives, including corporate finance (process for raising funds, managing funds raised, and maximizing corporate value).

Until now, small- and medium-sized enterprises primarily raised funds through bank loans, which could only be obtained after a time-consuming efforts based on trial balance sheets and financial statements. In the new FinTech era, these transactions take the form of business loan servicing based on accounting transactions, under which loans are provided after an extremely quick screening based on real-time account data (transaction). With freee, functions that make it convenient to raise funds at an appropriate time, at minimal cost, and of an optimal amount (including business loan servicing based on accounting transactions) are defined, collectively, as smart finance engines, and we are moving forward with their development and expedited deployment.

We achieved a symbolic milestone in October 2016, when Japan Net Bank began conducting finance screening using accounting freee data. Potential borrowers completed online applications, and the screening results were provided as soon as the same day. The financing was provided on the following business day. We view this as a breakthrough.

Furthermore, the general financing process does not end with applying and screening but includes a (currently) costly monitoring process. For these operations, the use of data provides benefits that take such forms as auto alerts. In particular, increasing the efficiency of qualitative monitoring operations for regional financial institutions makes it possible for sales staff to focus on more potentially lucrative activities, such as consulting for borrowers and implementation of deeper relationship banking.

YK: What is the future outlook?

DS: In 10 years, what form will the back office and finance of small- and medium-sized enterprises take? All back-office operations of small- and medium-sized enterprises will be interconnected via the Internet. The world of ERP and EDI, which major corporations have spent massive amounts of money to build, is becoming more democratized due to the power of the Internet and will become common even in small- and medium-sized enterprises. This is a world in which all operations use data, and AI, which learns from stored data, automates basic work, and automatically detects errors and mistakes. The payment flow will be automated to the greatest extent possible, and AI algorithms are likely to be utilized to identify optimal payment methods.

From the finance perspective, AI will play a major role, based on automated managerial accounting reports. Of course, concrete actions will include fund-raising. AI will be used to inform managers as to the optimal nature and timing of fund-raising activities.

freee makes it possible to conduct all processes in the cloud and to accumulate data in order to achieve ideal future outcomes. For financial institutions, freee is a small-business platform that not only enhances the Internet channel but also creates new financial products, and makes optimal recommendations for use of those products.

UX/UI

Goodpatch Inc.
Representative: Nao Tsuchiya, Director, President, and CEO
Company profile
Founded: 2011
Users: 48,000 people (as of December 2015)
Partners: SoftBank, Money Forward, Gunosy, BizReach
Goodpatch is a multi-device application design company. It is unique in that it provides a wide range of services that extend from the concept planning stage, to UX/UI design, prototype creation, UI patterns, user testing, and implementation–all under one roof.

Yoshitaka Kitao: Tell us about the history of the company.
Nao Tsuchiya: We are slightly different than the other companies included in this book because we are a design enterprise that specializes in the fields of user interface (UI) and user experience (UX). We are not a financial services–related company.

In recent years, the concepts of FinTech and design have drawn attention, but before looking at these trends, I would like to explain why I founded Goodpatch and launched a business centered on UI/UX.

In March 2011, I resigned from the web design company for which I was working and moved to San Francisco. Working as an intern at a design company in that city gave me the opportunity to interact with professionals at Silicon Valley startup companies. This changed my life.

In 2011, three years after Apple released the iPhone, smartphone use was spreading strongly, and even in San Francisco, there was a rapid increase in the number of startup companies with businesses centered on smartphone apps. Of course, there was a similar increase in the number of companies creating apps in Japan, but there was a vast difference between Japan and San Francisco in terms of the sophistication of the design and development processes. When Japanese companies create apps, they cram in numerous functions at the outset, and design and ease of use for users is of secondary importance.

By contrast, the startup companies in San Francisco started by designing the user experience, and dropped superfluous functions. They favored simple designs and focused on UI design from the beta stage onward. Furthermore, there is sure to be a designer on the management team, and all team members understand the importance of this function. When I saw this, I felt that it was important that Japanese companies also focus on UI and UX when designing services. After returning to Japan, I launched Goodpatch as a company that specializes in UI design. That was in September 2011. We were involved in the development of corporate services not merely as a design company but also as a deeply committed team member.

We launched operations five years ago and have opened offices in Tokyo, Berlin, and Taiwan as a leading planner in the field of UI/UX design, and have become a growth company with more than 100 employees.

YK: What are the distinguishing features of the business environment?
NT: Over the past couple of years, the importance of design, particularly that of UI/UX, has come into focus along with the concept of FinTech. We have helped several Japan-based FinTech companies, such as Money Forward and Nikkei Group's Quick, with design. In particular, when we were still a startup company with about 10 employees, we became involved with Money Forward. We took part in updating the UI, and the user experience dramatically improved. Now more than 5 million people use the service. The company has grown into one with more than 200 employees, and has become a leading FinTech company in Japan. Because of our involvement in the initial app, Money Forward recognized the importance of design and it even established a design strategy office.

Because there is greater activity related to FinTech and design in the United States and Europe, US-based Capital One, a major financial company, purchased the design firm Adaptive Path in 2014, which was a decisive event in this trend. Adaptive Path was regarded as an extremely renowned company in the UX design industry, so this acquisition news generated a lot of buzz in the industry. The management of Capital One was probably aware of the importance of design strategy and acquired the company because of the FinTech surge that appeared to be forming. In the United States, there have been numerous services that have dramatically altered what is considered common sense for financial services over the past several years, and all these services stress design strategy.

Misunderstanding of Design

NT: Before discussing design, I would like to dispel misunderstandings that many Japanese have on this topic. Many Japanese, when they hear the word *design*, envision visual decoration. But the utility of design extends well beyond optics. It includes factors that are not visible, such as how well users are known, to what extent things that users demand are created, the user experience design process, prototyping, and organization.

        In fact, design was not originally about developing visual appearance. Rather, it is a strategy intended to understand who the products and services are for and why, and the process of creating those products and services. Design education is more advanced in Europe and the United States than in Japan, and in new fields such as FinTech, the importance of UX design is more easily spread in those regions.

Disrupting the Market through the Spread of the Smartphone

NT: In ways that extend beyond FinTech, the spread of smartphones has dramatically changed the world over the past 10 years. The advent of smartphones has not only devastated numerous existing markets, but also resulted in the creation of new markets. People's lives have dramatically changed because of the advent of the smartphone. Previous to this, it was a given that people would connect to the Internet from desktop computers at home, their workplace, or school. The smartphone enabled connectivity whenever and wherever, even when on a train. Communication methods have grown more diverse because of various apps, and the obstacles to communication between users and companies have been reduced.

        Offerings such as the mobile payment service Square, which went public last year, could not have been created without the smartphones. The company proposed a new payment method using smartphones, which dramatically reduces the obstacles to payments between companies and users. The founder of Square, Jack Dorsey, quickly focused on the design aspects of the product because he wanted Square to become a product trusted by users.

Birth of Services from a User Perspective

NT: For many years, financial services was not a user-friendly business. That may be true of Japan even now. In general, to use financial services, it is necessary to have a bank or securities company account. Furthermore, the various financial services are complex and difficult to understand, creating major obstacles to their use. Young people dislike going to banks and securities companies, and consider it bothersome to gain an understanding of complex services. Young people in the past were probably the same.

　　　In recent years, the concept of robo-advisors, in which artificial intelligence helps manage assets, has developed. In the United States, the robo-advisors service is rapidly improving, and even in Japan, there is a trend toward AI-assisted asset management. Robo-advisor service, which is oriented toward the needs of younger people previously ignored by the industry, makes it possible to check asset-management performance via Internet and smartphone without visiting a branch office and it entails extremely low costs. It is a service geared for users.

　　　Incorporating the user perspective has become more important for financial services in recent years.

Easy-to-Use UI Improves UX

YK: Tell us how the business is progressing.

NT: An extremely important factor for improving user experience is the ease of using the UI. That is our major strength. In recent years, UI and UX have often been considered equivalent, but this is completely different than the original concept. Even so, the ease of use has a major impact on user experience.

　　　When we redesigned the Money Forward app, the old app was overflowing with information, and we struggled to find the items that users actually wanted. We prioritized information, put items into categories, reviewed the content, and limited information display to what users could see at a single glance.

　　　After the update, the number of positive reviews of the app grew steadily and featured comments that praised the increased ease of use. This resulted in an 11% increase in KPI. Money

Forward then won the 2014 Good Design award. We are no longer involved in the project, but Money Forward continues to capture more users.

US-based FinTech startup companies understand that the UI design has a major impact on UX, and they put a lot of energy into UI from the beginning. Some of the distinguishing features of the hot Silicon Valley–based startup Robinhood, a securites company, is that it offers trading services for free and all of its services are provided through the app. Another major distinguishing feature is that its UI is extremely easy to use. Stocks can be traded in a mere three steps. It appears that around 25% of Robinhood users are first-time traders, and the fact that the company makes it possible to easily use complex financial services is why it is supported by young people. Easy-to-use services lower obstacles for beginners, and is why it results in greater customer engagement than other complicated services. Therefore, putting energy into UI is extremely important.

Importance of the Organization Understanding Design

YK: What is the future outlook?

NT: I have mentioned how important design is for FinTech, but this is an extremely complex concept for financial organizations to understand. Many financial companies have little understanding of design, and even if they believe design is important for a service, the in-house understanding is that this refers to the visual aspects of the service. But simply having a nice visual design does not dramatically improve user experience.

In terms of promoting an understanding of design within an organization, consider again Capital One's purchase of Adaptive Path. Throughout the world, there are few cases of companies not outsourcing design-related work to a service provider with a reputation for UX; completely incorporating a design culture into a company is rare. It has been less than two years since the acquisition, but there has been some Internet reporting on Capital One's design-related efforts. A culture of conducting people-centered design and valuing feedback from customers has spread throughout the company, allowing them to uncover hard-to-find needs and transform them into services.

In Japan, there is yet to be such an acquisition of a design company by a major company, which is extremely regrettable.

There are concerns that Japanese companies will fall behind global companies that stress design strategy. Companies that see potential in design should probably move quickly.

CHAPTER 5

Issues for Financial Institutions and the Legal System

Current State of and Issues for Banks

In April 2013, the Bank of Japan (BOJ) adopted a policy of "unprecedented monetary easing": an approach that went so far as to push interest rates into negative territory by February 2016. This had a major impact on the asset composition and earnings structure of Japanese banks and brought to light various business issues.

In the first part of this chapter, I compare the performance of major Japanese banks against that of their regional counterparts, and then summarize their current state and the issues faced by Japanese banks. Then, in the second part, I focus on regional banks and suggest the direction in which I believe that their business should move.

Deposit-Loan Gap Remains 20% of Total Assets

First, let's take a look at changes in the composition of banks' balance sheets. As of March 31, 2017, the top four line items on Japanese banks' asset inventories were: (1) deposits (749.6 trillion yen), (2) loans (496.4 trillion yen), (3) securities (211.34 trillion yen), and (4) receivables from banks (211.33 trillion yen). From there, we see a major drop-off to the fifth largest asset category: trading assets (52.7 trillion yen gap).

The four main items, as well as the deposit-loan gap (deposits minus loans) as a percentage of total assets, are shown in Figure 5.1. There has been a major increase in the size of receivables from banks as a percentage of total assets for major and regional financial institutions. This is primarily due to excess reserves at the BOJ, which totaled 197.4 trillion yen in March 2017, 93% of which is due from banks. I consider the deposit-loan gap as a percentage of total assets to be the barometer of the banking industry, and

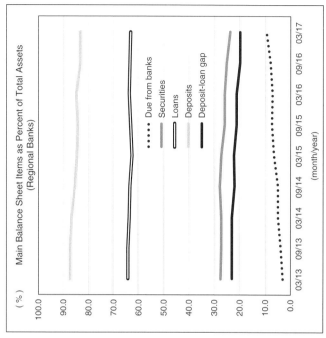

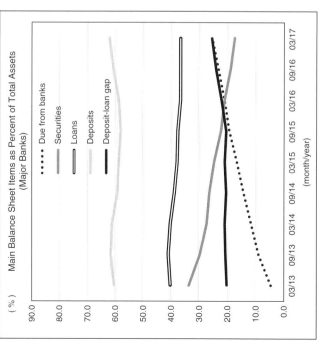

FIGURE 5.1 Main Balance Sheet Items as Percent of Total Assets

Source: Assets and liabilities of domestically licensed banks released by the BOJ.

I focus on that metric. For major banks, the deposit-loan gap as a percentage of total assets continued to increase (deteriorate) following the introduction of unprecedented monetary easing and topped it 25% for the fiscal year ended March 2017. For regional banks, the figure gradually declined (improved) but is still about 20% of total assets. In this way, excess reserves are simply accumulating on the balance sheets of Japanese banks, and there are no firm signs of a recovery from the hypothermia that has inflicted the vital banking system.

Growing Instability in Bank Earnings

I would like to now look at changes in income/losses for Japanese banks themselves. Table 5.1 provides a comparison of the main items in the fiscal year ended March 2013, before the policy of unprecedented monetary easing was introduced, and at the fiscal year ended March 2017. For major banks, both ordinary and net income fell between these periods. On the other hand, regional banks saw both ordinary and net income increase.

However, income from core operations (net interest income from deposits and loans+net fees and commissions on domestic and foreign exchange)–the fruit of banks' primary operations (financial intermediation, credit creation, and payments) and their most stable form of income–fell for both types of banks, but the decline for regional banks was particularly large. Nonrecurring gains (losses), which is highly variable and increased for both types of institutions.

Item	Major banks				Regional banks			
	FY 3/13	FY 3/17	Change	% change	FY 3/13	FY 3/17	Change	% change
	(trillion yen)	(trillion yen)	(trillion yen)	(%)	(trillion yen)	(trillion yen)	(trillion yen)	(%)
Net ordinary income	2.75	2.58	−0.17	−6.2	1.24	1.37	0.13	10.5
Net income	2.26	1.97	−0.29	−12.7	0.77	0.97	0.19	24.9
Net interest income from deposits and loans (A)	3.22	3.06	−0.17	−5.1	3.18	2.81	−0.37	−11.5
Net fees and commissions on domestic and foreign exchange (B)	0.29	0.31	0.02	6.4	0.21	0.20	−0.01	−4.9
Income from core operations (A+B)	3.52	3.37	−0.15	−4.2	3.38	3.01	−0.38	−11.1
Stocks (C)3 account balance	−0.23	0.50	0.73	--	−0.08	0.21	0.29	--
Bonds (D)5 account balance	0.76	0.10	−0.67	−87.4	0.19	−0.04	−0.23	−119.0
Loss on disposal of bad loans (E)	−0.20	−0.16	0.04	−19.4	−0.40	−0.06	0.35	−86.3
Total nonrecurring gains (losses) (C+D+E)	0.33	0.43	0.10	30.6	−0.29	0.12	0.41	--

TABLE 5.1 **Main Income Items**
Source: Graph based on data from analysis of financial statements of Japanese banks released by the Japanese Bankers Association.

This trend was not limited to the fiscal year ended March 2017, but has been in place for both types of banks since the introduction of unprecedented monetary easing (Figures 5.2 and 5.3). It is my opinion that instability in banks' income increased further after the introduction of this monetary policy.

Growing Gap between Net Assets and Shareholders' Equity

I would also like to examine the breakdown of net assets for banks themselves, and ROE for both types of banks (Figure 5.4). For the fiscal year ended March 2017, the ROE for major banks was 5.9%, while that for regional banks was only 4.5%. The main reason for the decline in ROE in the fiscal year ended March 2017 was the industrywide fall in net income, which is largely attributable to the deteriorating environment brought about by the introduction of the negative interest rate policy.

Total valuation, translation adjustments, and so on as a percentage of net assets as of March 31, 2017, was slightly less than 20% for both major and regional banks, and for Japanese banks, there is a large gap between shareholders' equity, "real equity," and net assets. This means that net assets are strongly impacted by the market environment.

For Three Major Japanese Financial Groups, International Operations and Group Companies Make Large Contributions to Earnings

Here, I would like to summarize the distinguishing aspects of earnings for the three major financial groups, each of which has a strong presence in Japan's financial industry.

The decline in income from core operations for major banks (−4.2%) was relatively small compared to that of regional banks (−11.1%) because of contributions from the international operations of the three major financial groups. Gross income from international operations for the core banks of the three major financial groups totaled 1.78 trillion yen for the fiscal year ended March 2017, of which 899.1 billion yen was interest income, and international operations contributed 37.2% of total gross income and 30.8% of total net interest income from domestic and international operations.

Furthermore, net income attributable to parent company shareholders for the three major financial groups totaled 2.24 trillion yen, which is 1.49 times the 1.51 trillion yen in total net income for the three banks of those financial groups. The international operations and their strong contributions to group company earnings have clearly become a difference between the earnings structure of the three major financial groups and that of banks centered on domestic banking operations (which are primarily regional banks) over the past several years.

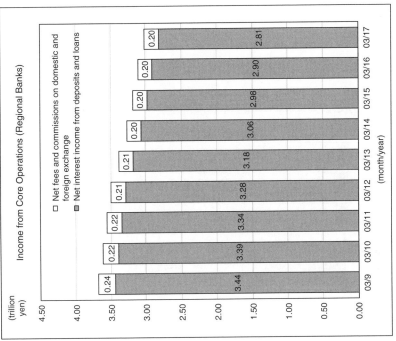

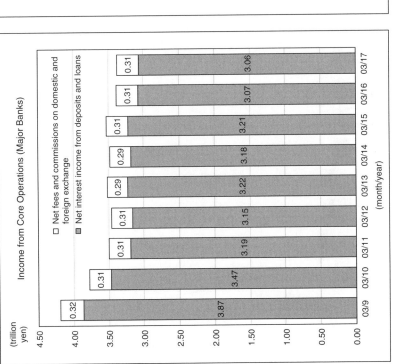

FIGURE 5.2 Income from Core Operations

Source: Graph based on data from analysis of financial statements of Japanese banks released by the Japanese Bankers Association.

137

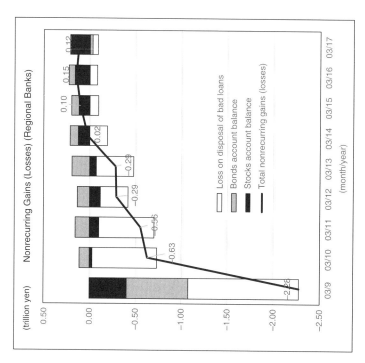

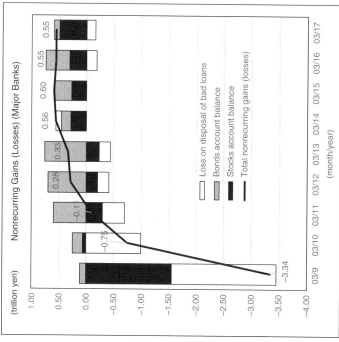

FIGURE 5.3 Nonrecurring Gains (Losses)

Source: Graph based on data from analysis of financial statements of Japanese Banks released by the Japanese Bankers Association and status of nonperforming loans by the Financial Services Agency.

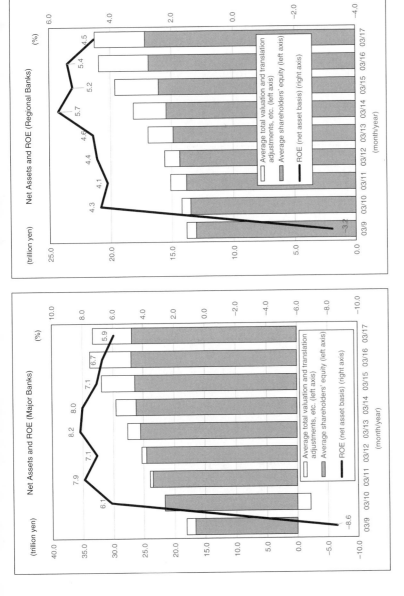

FIGURE 5.4 Breakdown of Net Assets and ROE

Note. Average shareholders' equity and total valuation and translation adjustments, etc., is the simple averaged balance of the beginning of the period (end of the previous fiscal year) and end of the fiscal year. ROE (net asset basis) is calculated by dividing net income by the total of average shareholders' equity and average total valuation and translation adjustments, etc. *Source:* Graph based on data from analysis of financial statements of Japanese banks released by the Japanese Bankers Association.

Future of Regional Banks

Growing Importance of Regional Banks in Japan's Financial System

I would now like to summarize current and future business issues for regional banks, whose operations are primarily domestic operations. Regional banks' share of deposits, loans, and branch offices is shown in Table 5.2.

Looking at the total for tier 1 and tier 2 regional banks reveals that they account for 27.7% of deposits and 40.8% of loans. Their share of both these financial categories has increased over the past 10 years, with their share of loans rising 4.6 percentage points. This clearly shows that for the regional economies of Japan, the importance of regional banks is steadily growing.

	Regional banks Type	Regional banks' share of financial industry total, etc.					
		Deposits (trillion yen)	Deposits share (%)	Loans (trillion yen)	Loans share (%)	Branch offices	Branch offices share (%)
March 31, 2006	Tier 1 regional banks	193	19.7	141	28.0	7,394	12.4
	Tier 2 regional banks	55	5.6	41	8.2	3,275	5.5
	All regional banks	247	25.2	182	36.2	10,669	18.0
March 31, 2016	Tier 1 regional banks	257	22.0	185	32.2	7,428	13.2
	Tier 2 regional banks	66	5.7	49	8.6	2,968	5.3
	All regional banks	323	27.7	234	40.8	10,396	18.4
% change over 10 years	Tier 1 regional banks	33.2	2.4	31.2	4.2	0.5	0.7
Change in share described by percentage points	Tier 2 regional banks	21.8	0.1	19.1	0.4	−9.4	−0.3
	All regional banks	30.7	2.5	28.4	4.6	−2.6	0.5

TABLE 5.2 Regional Banks' Deposits, Loans, and Number of Offices as Percentage of Total of the Overall Financial Industry
Source: Based on data from *Financial Map* issued by Financial Journal Co., Ltd.

Expected Narrowing of Earnings from Lending Operations

Figure 5.5 gives a more detailed look at the earnings structure of regional banks for the fiscal year ended March 2017. A distinguishing feature of regional banks is that interest and dividends from securities and net interest income from deposits and loans, which are directly impacted by the BOJ's negative interest rate policy, account for 82% of ordinary income.

Figure 5.6 shows an overview of changes in the profitability of lending operations for tier 1 and tier 2 regional banks after the introduction of unprecedented monetary easing. The year-on-year percentage change in

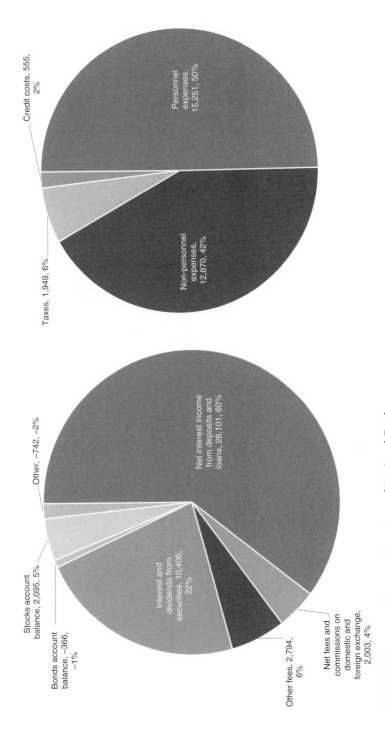

FIGURE 5.5 Income/Expense Structure of Regional Banks
Source: Graph based on data from analysis of financial statements of Japanese banks released by the Japanese Bankers Association.

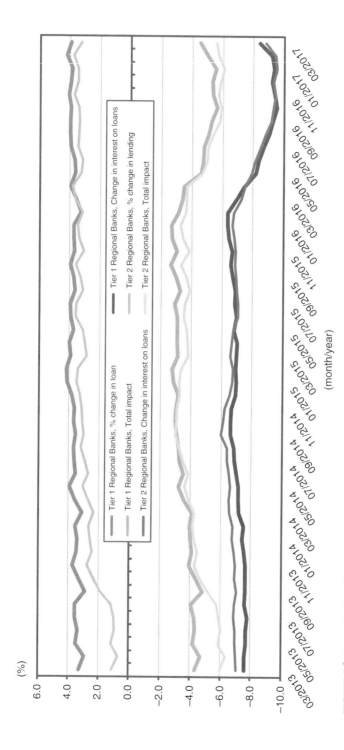

FIGURE 5.6 Profitability of Lending Operations of Regional Banks

Source: Assets and liabilities of domestically licensed banks released by the BOJ.

outstanding balance of loans is given as the volume impact, price impact is the year-on-year percentage change in the average contracted interest rate (stock basis), and the sum of these as the total impact.

Although the change in lending was in the upper 3%–range even after the negative interest rate policy was introduced in February 2016, the contracted interest rate (stock basis) on new loans rapidly fell following the introduction of that policy, which resulted in the recent decline – amounting to an amount in excess of 8%.

Because the decline for January 2016 was only about 6%, the negative interest rate policy has had a major impact, as indicated in the graph.

Many Factors Causing Earnings Uncertainty

Furthermore, of the almost 1.04 trillion yen in interest and dividends from securities, it is estimated that about 300.0 billion yen are gains from the termination of privately placed investment trusts (actual capital gain on bonds and stocks), and there is the risk that this could substantially fall – particularly if certain market conditions manifest themselves.

Let's now look at operating expenses. According to Tokyo Shoko Research, the number of corporate bankruptcies for the 2016 calendar year fell 4.2% year on year and total liabilities of bankrupt companies declined 5.0%. For now, there is probably little concern about a dramatic increase in credit costs; regional banks' loss on disposal of bad loans as a percentage of total credit, following the collapse of Lehman Brothers (FY2009 – FY2015), was on average 0.16%.

If credit costs were to reach the same level for large international banks, the total amount would approach 400 billion yen, which is dramatically greater than the 55.5 billion yen for the fiscal year ended March 2017.

Difficulty of Dramatically Cutting Operating Expenses

It is not easy for a bank to dramatically cut operating expenses. For example, these expenditures for the fiscal year ended March 2017 were about the same as those for the previous fiscal year. It is estimated that system expenses account for a little less than 20% of operating costs. According to a survey of regional banks conducted by the Center for Financial Industry Information Systems (FISC), system-related spending by all regional banks is about 500 – 510 billion yen annually, and a trial calculation indicates that about 70% of that is for maintenance (approximately 30% is strategic and prospective investments). These costs, therefore, are a heavy burden for banks.

As of the fiscal year ended March 2017, there was a difference between ordinary income and ordinary expenses (i.e., net ordinary income) of slightly less than 1.37 trillion yen, and just under 70% of that would be lost if net interest income from deposits and loans and interest and dividends from securities fell 15%, and credit costs of 0.16% actually were to be realized (a completely realistic scenario).

Market's Valuation of Regional Bank Stocks Remains Harsh

Market valuation of all listed regional banks has deteriorated as their earnings outlook weakened following the introduction of negative interest rates. Total market value of all listed regional banks precipitously fell 37%, from 13 trillion yen at its peak to 8.1 trillion yen at the end of June 2016. Over that period, average real PBR declined to 0.39 times from 0.57 times, and regional banks were sold off to such a degree that doubts about the going concern assumption arose in the market.

Stock markets subsequently recovered, and the share price of regional banks rebounded with their total market value as of the end of March 2017 increasing to 10.8 trillion yen (a 16% decline compared to the end of December 2015), and average PBR improving to 0.5 times. A majority of listed regional banks, however, have a PBR well below this threshold, and the market assessment of regional banks is not optimistic.

Need for a Strategy That Leads to a Fundamental Review of the Earnings

Well, what is required of regional banks in the future?

A top priority is a fundamental review of the earnings structure shown in Figure 5.7. The data suggests that a full paradigm shift (not simply adjustments to existing policies) is probably necessary. If banks merge, it will probably involve a massive consolidation of branch offices, and that will directly lead to an improvement in business efficiency.

Another scenario is for banks to choose to cooperate, not compete, with FinTech startup companies, including efforts to increase income by expanding customer reach and to cut costs by introducing innovative business process re-engineering (BPR).

I expect and hope that the Financial System Working Group, which is discussing the Ideal Financial Group System WG Group Report (December 2015), along with amendments to the Banking Act, which were subsequently quickly implemented, will approve this direction for Japanese banks. However, it would take many years to reap major benefits from either merger of regional banks or cooperation with FinTech startup companies. During that time, regional banks, which are stock companies, would have to strive to implement limited measures to increase earning and improve market valuations – all under the harsh business conditions of negative interest rates.

There are several ways to communicate to the market that management has dramatically changed. One way is to work to fundamentally unwind cross-shareholding among regional banks, an initiative which has progressed at a snail's pace. In the *yukashoken hokokusho* (securities reports) for the fiscal year ended March 2016, there are 70 regional banks and holding companies who list the shares of regional banks as major designated equity instruments, and almost 230 regional banks hold these shares.

This shows the hollowing out of capital (double gearing) in Japan's regional financial system. Furthermore, the Abe government has positioned corporate governance reforms as an important public policy initiative. Regional banks should shed their tradition of cross-shareholdings as passive shareholders. They should actively strive to reduce strategic stock holdings, particularly of banks, and improve the quality of capital by realizing capital gains and losses. It is my opinion that a scenario of regional banks fundamentally revising their capital policy in some way, such as setting a rational optimal capital level, is fully worth examining – at least so long as negative interest rates ensue.

Required Regulations

FinTech Lowers Barriers between Financial Industry and Other Industries

FinTech will generate major changes in broadly defined financial businesses by attracting companies from other industries throughout the world. When one speaks of FinTech, the topics that draw most of the attention are cryptocurrencies such as Bitcoin, and investments in startup companies. FinTech, however, will probably cause structural changes across many fields of business operation. Of those changes, the greatest one will be a lowering of barriers between the financial industry and other industries.

The information technology (IT) revolution will probably evolve into an artificial intelligence (AI) breakthrough. This may eliminate the need for various elements of the financial industry, including large amounts of capital, large numbers of workers, massive system investments, and networks centered on branch offices and ATMs. As the size of required new investments declines, companies in other industries will face lower barriers to enter the financial services industry.

The number of business enterprises that enter the financial services industry, therefore, will probably increase. Sony has added Sony Bank to its group, and Seven & I Holdings has Seven Bank. Lawsons is also moving forward with plans to establish a bank, and more and more companies in other industries may enter the financial industry.

In this way, fundamental structural reforms are occurring in the financial industry. It is only natural that new rules, including ones from the perspective of global financial regulation in response to these reforms, will have to be created.

Stricter Global Financial Regulation

Shadow banking, which is difficult to regulate and supervise, was undoubtedly one of the main causes of the collapse of Lehman Brothers, as well as the demise of nonbank financial service enterprises, and of the credit crisis in general. Beyond Lehman Brothers, well-known victims of the crash include the major insurance company American International Group (AIG), the Federal National Mortgage Association (FNMA), and structured investment vehicles (SIVs) of major financial institutions. These failures brought about various responses, including an infusion of public funds into major financial institutions in Europe and the United States.

In response, leading countries throughout the world started to reform financial regulation. In 2008, the first meeting of the heads of the 20 leading economies (G20 Summit) was held in Washington, DC, and at the 2009 G20 Summit in London, this group established the basic policy for global financial regulation reform.

Examples of greater global financial regulations after the collapse of Lehman Brothers include stricter designation and supervision of global, systemically important financial institutions (G-SIFIs); stricter capital regulations; introduction of liquidity regulations (Basel III); regulation of over-the-counter derivatives; reforms to the compensation system for managers of financial institutions; reforms to the international accounting system (IFRS); and stronger monitoring and supervision of the shadow banking industry.

The formulation of global financial regulatory measures peaks at the G20 Summit, which leaders of various countries attended. Now, the Financial Stability Board (FSB) Forum takes the lead in global efforts to reform financial regulation. Regarding setting detailed rules in each field, various bodies, including the Basel Committee on Banking Supervision (BCBS), the International Organization of Securities Commissions (IOSCO), International Association of Insurance Supervisors (IAIS), and International Accounting Standards Board (IASB) do so in response to FSB requests. For example, the BCBS formulated Basel III reforms: capital regulations for banks.

The regulations and rules set by these entities are given legal force by each country, creating hard laws. In Japan, this is primarily the responsibility of the Financial Services Agency.

Withdrawal of Business Enterprises from the Finance Business in the United States

In the United States, the Dodd–Frank Wall Street Reform and Consumer Protection Act (Dodd–Frank Act) gave the Federal Reserve Board (FRB) the authority not only to supervise not only major bank groups, but also nonbank financial institutions through accreditation by the Financial Stability Oversight Council (FSOC).

Although the Securities and Exchange Commission (SEC) possesses the authority to supervise securities companies, it lacks the means to save these entities through or other options. Therefore, major investment banks such as Goldman Sachs and Morgan Stanley obtained banking licenses, and were placed under the supervision of the Federal Reserve Board (FRB) at the time of the collapse of Lehman Brothers.

If only banks are subject to strict regulation, as has traditionally been the case, investment banks may relinquish their banking licenses. In that case, there would be fewer ways to save nonbank financial institutions. Therefore, even if companies surrender their banking licenses, ones that fall under the Troubled Asset Relief Program (TARP), because they have assets of at least $50 billion (as of January 1, 2010), are subject to regulation (also known as the "Hotel California" provision in Dodd–Frank Act).

The Dodd–Frank Act strengthened regulation of entry into the banking industry by companies in other industries. Companies with large-scale financial businesses fall under the supervision of the Federal Reserve Board, and are subject to certain regulations, such as capital requirements, stress tests and creation of a living will (plan to dissolve the business in the case of a bankruptcy).

Therefore, some companies that had massive financial businesses, such as General Electric (GE), have withdrawn from the financial business out of a desire to avoid associated regulations. In other words, even if FinTech makes it easy for business enterprises to enter the financial business, few companies will probably undertake banking operations involving deposits and financial operations that entail massive capital and regulation.

In the United States, business enterprises may enter the financial business in fields such as payments and remittances, which do not extensively use corporate assets. An example of this is Apple entering the payment business with its iPhone 7. Furthermore, IBM and Microsoft are focusing on efforts such as building a payment and remittance system using blockchain technology. In the United States, it would probably be difficult for businesses to enter the market by establishing or acquiring a banking, securities, or insurance subsidiary in the manner associated with Japan-based Sony Bank and Seven Bank.

Focus should be, however, on the Trump administration's efforts to amend the Dodd–Frank Act. During the presidential election campaign, President Trump promised to revise the act. Furthermore, the Republican

Party, which would like to amend the act, has a majority in both the upper and lower houses of Congress. It is, therefore, extremely likely that amendments will be made to the act.

The amendments, however, will probably be limited. There are several reasons for this. First, it would be harshly criticized by the public. People still remember the collapse of Lehman Brothers, and there would be strong opposition to elements that would be deemed to unilaterally benefit the financial industry and its high salaries. Revisions beneficial to the financial industry may also lead to charges that members of the Trump administration would be acting to benefit themselves, as many of the key figures in it are former managers of the major investment bank Goldman Sachs.

Second, major financial institutions do not necessarily endorse extensive amendments to the act. Since regulations such as Basel III, which form the core of financial regulations, are international rules, the United States cannot change them unilaterally. Regulations that are unique to the United States are de facto restrictions on the entry of business enterprises into the financial industry, as previously discussed. If those are eliminated, GE and GM may once again enter the financial industry. In that case, existing major financial institutions would face fiercer competition, which is not a prospect much to their liking.

In summary, even if there are revisions to the Dodd–Frank Act, they will probably not be major changes to the underlying framework.

Global Financial Regulation and FinTech

In Japan, the entry of business companies into the financial industry would be welcome. Taking into consideration lessons from the collapse of Lehman Brothers, it is clear, however, that completely free entry of business enterprises into the financial industry is not desirable. There is also a global trend toward stricter financial regulation, and Japan cannot just do what it wants in these areas.

For example, Sharp Corporation itself fell into financial difficulties and was ultimately acquired by a Taiwanese company. Let's assume Sharp had a Sharp Bank like Sony has Sony Bank. It would be best if rules regarding how to handle Sharp Bank in various situations, such as financial difficulties, were set in advance. In particular, a liquidation plan and measures that make it easy to sell off the business in the case of financial difficulties should be created during noncrisis time.

It is also important that regulatory authorities monitor the business of the bank's parent company. This does not mean that the Financial Services Agency should strictly supervise nonfinancial elements of business enterprises but that there is close communication during noncrisis times and a system to cooperatively respond when a crisis hits.

Laws must be developed for this type of regulation, and some are already in place, including the Financial Instruments and Exchange Act, Banking Act, and Deposit Insurance Act. In particular, it would be best to design the system using highly flexible so-called soft law because finance and AI experience rapid technological progress and changes.

Need to Develop a Multifaceted Legal System

For FinTech, it is necessary to establish new laws from the following perspectives because it is difficult to respond within the framework of current regulations. First, there is a need to provide more specific definitions for currencies. Crypto currencies, such as Bitcoin and electronic money, including Suica and T-points and cards, are rapidly spreading. Throughout the world, cryptocurrencies are evolving from the Bitcoin example, which the general public can purchase, to various other types of currencies including regional ones that only people in a particular region can use, and ones managed by a particular company (e.g., private blockchain instruments such as MUFG Coin). In the future, numerous cryptocurrencies will probably be created.

Concepts such as cryptocurrencies and electronic money are not subject to Bank of Japan (BOJ) policy. If they rapidly grow in scale, however, they will probably have a major impact on the currency policy of the entire country. Even if the BOJ moved to tighten monetary policy to fight inflation, the impact of such a move would be undermined if electronic money and cryptocurrencies were to significantly expand their reach.

It is important, therefore, to first create a system to compile statistics, protect consumers and achieve other objectives. Related laws include the Financial Instrument and Exchange Act, Bank of Japan Act, Foreign Exchange and Foreign Trade Act, and Payment Services Act. There are also concerns that Bitcoins could be used to launder money, so related regulations are necessary. The Act on Prevention of Transfer of Criminal Proceeds is one example of this.

Second, there is the perspective of acts that target particular industries, such as the financial services industry. These include the Financial Services and Exchange Act, Banking Act, Insurance Act, Payment Services Act, Installment Sales Act, and Money Lending Business Act. In 2016, the Banking Act, Agricultural Co-operatives Act, Electronically Recorded Monetary Claims Act, and Financial Services Act were partially amended to respond to changes in the environment, such as advances in telecommunication technology. In the future, as technology evolves, it will probably be necessary to revise several finance related laws.

Third, there is the perspective of international business. Because financial markets are growing more global and FinTech is spreading throughout the world, it is important to think about things from a global perspective.

The financial services industry is global, and this could impact legal structures including the Foreign Exchange and Foreign Trade Act. Furthermore, if payments are made in dollars and money is remitted to foreign countries through US-based financial institutions, it could lead to violations of US laws. In that case, participating entities could be subject to US penalties. It is probably important, therefore, to consider laws related to international payments and remittances, particularly for the United States, including the anti-money–laundering laws.

Because of this, it is necessary to have constructive discussions on developing a Japanese corporate and legal system for FinTech. In particular, it is hoped that working with the Financial Stability Board (FSB), Japan will play a leading role in creating an efficient, flexible, and well-adapted set of global rules.

Afterword

The world now has an opportunity to undergo a major transition that could be considered the fourth industrial revolution. The changes are such that they extend beyond mere technical innovation and can truly be called a revolution. Viewed in their totality, these changes will fundamentally alter the structure of society as technology progresses on a scale never before experienced. A leading example of this is FinTech, an industrial revolution transpiring in the financial industry.

This may seem somewhat unrelated, but there was an interesting debate at the 2016 World Economic Forum, where it was questioned was whether the world is now at war or peace. This seemingly simple question is actually quite difficult to answer and experts came to the conclusion that they do not know. According to old definitions, war exists when the infrastructure called an army is put into play. However, new technologies are evolving, and it is possible to attack a party even without resorting to that traditional infrastructure, because war can take the form of cyberterrorism and terrorism.

In fact, similar problems are occurring in all aspects of the economy. In general, the fourth industrial revolution is making the various systems and social infrastructure that we have built up until now unnecessary.

For example, until now, a citywide infrastructure of taxi cabs was necessary if one wanted to get safely from point A to point B, with peace of mind, in most major cities. If someone outside that infrastructure gave me a ride, he or she could take me anywhere and charge an exorbitant fare. However, taxi businesses that operate within the system called the established industry, are sanctioned by the government and cars are required to have meters; if there is a problem, I can submit a complaint. The social infrastructure of authorized taxis has been beneficial for consumers.

However, a new system that makes it possible to get around through ridesharing is now spreading throughout the world, and it is now possible to evaluate whether a driver is competent and safe using big data provided by smartphones. Even if it is not officially a taxi, individuals can judge whether the service, even if it is not an official taxi, is good or not by using big data. A perfect example of this is Uber, whose corporate value has grown to 7 trillion yen ($66B), or about one-third that of Toyota, the company that boasts the largest corporate value in Japan.

Similarly, there is Airbnb, a company that realizes a sharing economy in the private lodging field, whose corporate value has grown to 3 trillion yen ($28B), which is greater than half the major banks in Japan. In other words, Uber is not part of the taxi industry and Airbnb is not in the hotel industry, but one could say that they are in the social networking industry.

The phenomenon of infrastructure becoming unnecessary could also occur in the financial industry. In the past, the infrastructure referred to as banks was necessary, but IT companies such as Amazon and Google, which possess big data, can now handle common operations such as payments. Furthermore, linking AI to IoT is leading to a growing range of completely new business opportunities. This new phenomenon is generally called *FinTech*, and countries throughout the world are competing and creating opportunities related to how FinTech will evolve. The question becomes how the various perspectives and ventures discussed in this book will be realized.

Depending on how you look at it, FinTech also possesses aspects that reject the existing financial industry. Although there are hopes that Japanese financial institutions will play an active role in this field, one can probably argue that it will be a major test as to whether they can really break out of their former shell, and boldly promote FinTech.

In the Japanese government's growth strategy, adopted by the cabinet in 2016, the policies related to FinTech were woefully insufficient. In the 2017 growth strategy, however, a regulatory sandbox method was adopted as a new way to implement deregulation. This is a mechanism that financial regulatory authorities in England and Singapore created to support new FinTech companies, and it is expected that this will result in dramatic progress in FinTech in Japan as well. The philosophy could be stated as follows: *Forget past rules and regulations. Freely attempt things on a trial-and-error basis.*

Although it was more than a decade ago, when I was responsible for the Japanese government's finance-related policy, I thought that both reactive and proactive types of reforms were required in this field. It goes without saying that at that time, reactive reforms were cleaning up the balance sheets of financial institutions—that is, disposing of nonperforming loans. There have been various debates, but Japanese financial institutions were able to accomplish this cleanup task in dramatic fashion over the 10 years after the collapse of the bubble. For various reasons, including that experience, Japanese financial institutions were probably able to better overcome the major problems faced by global financial institutions after the collapse of Lehman Brothers.

However, there continue to be various issues related to proactive reforms. During that time, there have been dramatic changes in global financial and economic conditions. In order to respond to these changes, Japan must substantively accelerate the speed of reforms. This means that there are now major economic opportunities – particularly as the 2020 Tokyo Olympic and Paralympic Games approach. These events are viewed by over 70% of the world's population. It is exactly because of this that there is a major opportunity to push forward with reforms before the games are held. I hope that the so-called deadline effect is leveraged to achieve dramatic progress in the field of FinTech.

Heizō Takenaka[1]

---

[1] For more information on Heizō Takenaka, see www.weforum.org/people/heizo-takenaka

About the Author and Editor

Yoshitaka Kitao

1951: Born in Hyogo Prefecture, Japan
1974: Graduated from Keio University, Japan, and joined Nomura Securities Co., Ltd
1978: Graduated from Cambridge University, England
1989: Executive director, Wasserstein Perella & Co. (London)
1992: Appointed Business Entity Division III Head, Nomura Securities Co., Ltd
1995: Appointed managing director of SoftBank Corporation
1999: Representative director, president, SoftBank Investment Corporation (currently SBI Holdings Inc.)

Present:
   Yoshitaka Kitao was appointed representative director, president, and CEO of SBI Holdings, Inc., which is an integrated business group that has developed a wide range of businesses with our group companies, including financial services such as securities, banking and insurance; asset management for the creation of new industries; and biotechnology-related business, such as pharmaceutical developments.
   He also is director of the SBI Children's Hope Foundation and president of SBI Graduate School, among other responsibilities.

Selected Publications
   Why Do We Work? (published by Chichi Publication); *The SBI Group Vision and Strategy: Continuously Evolving Management* (published by Toyo Keizai Inc./English language translation published by John Wiley & Sons, Inc.); *The Essence of the Words of Masahiro Yasuoka* (published by President Inc.).

Index